Most Certainly True

Most Certainly True

Sermons on Luther's Catechisms

MICHAEL KASTING

Foreword by John T. Pless

RESOURCE *Publications* · Eugene, Oregon

MOST CERTAINLY TRUE
Sermons on Luther's Catechisms

Copyright © 2024 Michael Kasting. All rights reserved. Except for brief quotations in critical publications or reviews, no part of this book may be reproduced in any manner without prior written permission from the publisher. Write: Permissions, Wipf and Stock Publishers, 199 W. 8th Ave., Suite 3, Eugene, OR 97401.

Resource Publications
An Imprint of Wipf and Stock Publishers
199 W. 8th Ave., Suite 3
Eugene, OR 97401

www.wipfandstock.com

PAPERBACK ISBN: 979-8-3852-2768-6
HARDCOVER ISBN: 979-8-3852-2769-3
EBOOK ISBN: 979-8-3852-2770-9

All Scripture citations in this volume, unless otherwise noted, are from

THE HOLY BIBLE, NEW INTERNATIONAL VERSION®, NIV® Copyright © 1973, 1978, 1984, 2011 by Biblica, Inc.® Used by permission. All rights reserved worldwide.

Scripture citations marked KJV are from the Authorized (King James) Version. Reproduced by permission of the Crown's patentee, Cambridge University Press.

Scripture citations marked RSV are from the Revised Standard Version of the Bible, copyright 1952 and 1971 by the Division of Christian Education of the National Council of the Churches of Christ in the United States of America. Used by permission. All rights reserved.

Select excerpts from Luther's Small Catechism with Explanation and Luther's Large Catechism appear in Commandments 1-10, Creed Sermons 2, 3, 5, 7, 9, 10, 12; Lord's Prayer Intro; Petitions 1, 2, 3, 4, 6, 7; Baptism Sermons 1, 2; Keys Sermon 1; and Holy Communion Sermon 2.

Small Catechism citations in this volume are taken from *Luther's Small Catechism with Explanation* © 1986 Concordia Publishing House. Used with permission. cph.org.

Large Catechism citations in this volume are taken from *Luther's Large Catechism* © 1978 Concordia Publishing House. Used with permission. cph.org.

Table of Contents

Foreword vii
Author's Preface xi

THE TEN COMMANDMENTS
  First Commandment – "No Other Gods" 3
  Second Commandment – "Using God's Name" 7
  Third commandment – "A Day for Remembering" 11
  Fourth Commandment – "Honor Your Parents" 15
  Fifth Commandment – "The Gift of Life" 19
  Sixth Commandment – "In Matters of Sex" 23
  Seventh Commandment – "A Parade of Thieves" 27
  Eighth Commandment – "My Neighbor's Good Name" 31
  Ninth and Tenth Commandments – "No Coveting!" 35

THE APOSTLES' CREED
  First Article
    "What Does it Mean to Believe?" 41
    "I Believe in God the Father" 46
  Second Article
    "I Believe in Jesus Christ" 51
    "I Believe in the Virgin Birth" 56
    "I Believe He Suffered and Died" 60
    "I Believe He Descended into Hell" 64
    "I Believe He Rose from the Dead" 68
    "I Believe in the Ascension" 73
    "I Believe in Judgment Day" 77

v

Third Article
  "I Believe in the Holy Spirit" 82
  "I Believe in the Church" 86
  "I Believe in the Life Everlasting" 91

THE LORD'S PRAYER
  Introduction – "Calling God 'Father'" 99
  First Petition – "Hallowed be Your Name" 103
  Second Petition – "Your Kingdom Come" 107
  Third Petition – "Your Will Be Done" 111
  Fourth Petition – "Our Daily Bread" 115
  Fifth Petition – "Forgive us, as we Forgive" 119
  Sixth Petition – "Lead us not into Temptation" 123
  Seventh Petition – "Deliver us from Evil" 127

THE SACRAMENT OF HOLY BAPTISM
  John 3:1–8 - "Born Again" 133
  Matt. 3:13–17 - "Christ's Baptism and Mine" 138

OFFICE OF THE KEYS (CONFESSION)
  Matthew 16:15–30 – "I Give You the Keys" 145
  Matthew 18:15 – "Tough Love" 150

THE SACRAMENT OF THE ALTAR
  1 Cor. 10:16-17 – "Holy Communion" 157
  1 Cor. 11:23-29 – "Getting Ready for the Supper" 161

Bibliography 165

Foreword

MARTIN LUTHER'S SMALL AND Large Catechisms were born in the pulpit. Years before Luther prepared his two catechisms, catechetical preaching was taking place as priests were instructed to preach on chief texts such as the Ten Commandments, the Apostles' Creed, and the Lord's Prayer to combat widespread biblical and doctrinal illiteracy among the common people. Even before Luther posted his Ninety-Five Theses, he was, like many of his peers, preaching "catechism sermons." We know that he preached such a sermon as early as July, 1516, well over a year before October 31, 1517.

In 1527, the Reformer would lament: "Daily I find that there are now only a few preachers who truly and correctly understand the Our Father, the Creed, and the Ten Commandments and who are able to teach them for the poor common people. All the same, they dash into Daniel, Hosea, John's Apocalypse, and other difficult books. The poor rabble are drawn in, listen to, and gawk at these jesters with great wonder. And when the year is through, they can still recite neither the Our Father, nor the Creed nor the Commandments. But it is these things that are the ancient, true Christian catechism or common education for Christians."[1] The Saxon Visitation of the following year would reveal the neediness of both Lutheran preachers and laity when it came to the knowledge of the basic components of the Christian faith, evoking this response from Luther: "The deplorable, wretched deprivation that I recently encountered while I was a visitor has constrained and compelled me to prepare this catechism, or Christian instruction, in such a brief, plain, and simple version."[2]

Luther's catechetical sermons of 1528 would form the basic content and contours of the Large Catechism. The Small Catechism is a distillation

---

1. Luther, Preface to Commentary on Zechariah, AE 20:156
2. Luther, "Preface to the Small Catechism" in *The Book of Concord*, ed. Robert Kolb and Timothy Wengert, Fortress Press, 2000, 347.

FOREWORD

of material from the Large Catechism. The two catechisms go hand in hand and function to guide both preachers in their proclamation of Christ and hearers in their understanding and appropriation of evangelical preaching. Catechism sermons emerged as a homiletical genre in 16th century Lutheranism. The Small Catechism functioned as a way of imparting to ordinary believers the chief things that a Christian should know in life and death.

Current Lutheran hymnals such as the *Lutheran Service Book* include the texts of the Small Catechism, Luther's catechetical hymns, and a liturgical order entitled, "Service of Prayer and Preaching" that includes recitation of parts of the Small Catechism and the provision for a sermon based on a part of the Catechism. In this way, the framers of this hymnal recognize the historical precedence for catechetical preaching.

Pastor Michael Kasting is building on a solid historical legacy in offering to the church his own catechetical sermons in *Most Certainly True*. His sermons, however, are not antique relics from the distant memory of the church that carries Luther's name. These sermons reckon with the fact that 21st century Christians are not unlike their 16th century counterparts. Doctrinal indifference and confusion to fundamental aspects of Christian faith and life are present in the thinking even of people who have grown up in the church. Spiritual amnesia is a constant threat under the acidity of secularity. Mythologies of human autonomy and untested assumptions about the power of human freedom abound. It is into this context that Pastor Kasting preaches, inviting his hearers to remember and meditate on the truthfulness of the work of the Triune God that Luther confessed with clarity and boldness in the Small Catechism.

Born out of many years of pastoral experience, Pastor Kasting lets readers listen in on and discover in these sermons not only models to be emulated in their own preaching, but thoughtful meditations for their own edification in the Gospel of God's favor made manifest in the word of the cross. Laity will find in these sermons a refresher course in things that they may have learned in confirmation class but have grown dim with the passage of time.

The great 20th century scholar of the Small Catechism, Albrecht Peters, observed, "From the beginning to the end of the world, God teaches the catechism, and His saints delight in remaining His pupils in this. How can we think that we have already mastered the catechism?"[3] Luther envisioned

---

3. Peters, *Commentary on Luther's Catechisms: Ten Commandments*, Concordia Publishing House, 2009, 26.

Foreword

Christians as "eternal pupils" of the Catechism, never graduating from a life of study, meditation, prayer, and cross-bearing until in death we commence to life with Christ forever in his heavenly kingdom. Along the way, we need preaching that works repentance and faith just as Luther outlined it in the Small Catechism.

In *Most Certainly True*, preachers and laity are treated to the fruits of Pastor Kasting's homiletical labors that will prompt a more fulsome use of the Small Catechism.

John T. Pless, M.Div.; D. Litt.
Concordia Theological Seminary
Fort Wayne, IN
Author of *Luther's Small Catechism: A Manual for Discipleship*
   and *Praying Luther's Small Catechism*

Author's Preface

I BECAME ACQUAINTED WITH the Small Catechism the way many other children did. Along with the Bible, it was the primary text my pastor used to instruct us in our Saturday morning confirmation classes. Week after week came a new memory assignment. "What does this mean?" was a steadily repeated refrain. A portion of the catechism, along with several Bible passages, was always on the menu. I studied dutifully, rising to the challenge.

When confirmation day arrived (Pentecost Sunday for us), we had a public examination before the congregation assembled for worship that day. We sat in chairs facing the nave and rose, two at a time, to answer what the pastor asked us.

Mercifully, he told us ahead of time what he would ask, but it was still a kind of trial by ordeal.

Did it stick? I cannot answer for others, but I found that many of Luther's simple explanations of the basics stayed with me. Bible passages learned years earlier would suddenly surface unexpectedly. Luther's simple-but-profound explanations and many of those Bible passages still do, more than 60 years after that memorable Sunday.

It was a good thing, too, for after that day, I rarely heard those memorized words again in church. The catechism was not recited in worship, and the pastors under whose preaching I later sat almost never preached on it. If I had not eventually entered the ministry and had it all reinforced by teaching it myself, I wonder if I would have remembered things so well. My experience with the five congregations I served tells me that even those people who spent hours memorizing as I did often discovered that time had washed much of it away.

Observers of the Lutheran Church today frequently opine that "preaching the catechism" has dwindled or even disappeared, and in some places catechesis itself has shriveled to a handful of sessions. Despite our almost universal literacy and our immersion in the information age, an increasing number of our laity are unfamiliar with the most elementary truths of the faith. Whether the reason for that is busyness or sheer slothfulness, the Large Catechism is unknown to most of our congregants, and many pastors rarely or never preach a series on these things Luther thought essential for people to know.

This present volume is an attempt to encourage the marriage of catechesis with homiletics. After the catechisms were published, Luther urged that pastors continue preaching on their content to strengthen the people's understanding. Lent was a season especially set apart for that endeavor. Convention notes from Missouri Synod Lutheran congregations in the 19th century reveal that such catechetical preaching was still widespread then, with some pastors covering the entire catechism annually!

I bring you a plea for a return to more substantive catechesis and more homiletical reinforcement of the same. How might a congregation use the catechisms? Let me list some possibilities.

First, the pastor, elders, and other leaders might make study of both catechisms together a priority for themselves. Second, the congregation would do well to procure sufficient copies of the Small Catechism for distribution to every home. Many hymnals already include it for use at church. Third, worship planners could set aside substantial time in regular worship for reciting portions of the catechisms, perhaps at the place where the Creed is normally spoken. Finally, the pastor could set a goal of preaching through the chief parts of the catechisms over several years (for example, the Ten Commandments in Year A, the Creed in Year B, the Lord's Prayer in Year C, and so on).

The sermons in this book are arranged according to the six chief parts as they appear in current editions of the Small Catechism. There are larger sections for the Ten Commandments, Creed, and Lord's Prayer, and smaller ones for Baptism, Confession (Office of the Keys), and the Sacrament of the Altar.

Though there are frequent citations from both catechisms, the sermons do not use the text of the catechisms so much as they seek to address the same topics, in some cases using sections of Scripture as the sermon texts.

Author's Preface

May the Lord of the Church encourage you, whether pastor, catechist, or layperson, to "grow in grace and in the knowledge of our Lord and Savior Jesus Christ" (2 Peter 3:18) and find joy in His service.

Michael Kasting
Pentecost Season, 2024

The Ten Commandments

The First Commandment – "No Other Gods"

Everyone knows the Ten Commandments. Don't they?

At least they used to. There was a time when the commandments were memorized by almost every school child and recited at public gatherings so that the entire population, even the unchurched, knew them.

Not so now! Recently someone guessed that even among churchgoers, fewer than one person in ten could list them all in order. If we tried it here and now, how would you do?

What has happened is not simply a neglect. It feels more like a revolt against the very idea that anyone in heaven or on earth has the right to tell us, "Thou shalt not!"

We humans may choose to revolt, but God has never revoked his commandments. These words, given long ago to Moses on Mt. Sinai, stand firm. Jesus himself said, "Until heaven and earth disappear, not the smallest letter, not the least stroke of a pen, will by any means disappear from the Law" (Matt 5:18).

Martin Luther placed the commandments at the head of his catechisms and said, "The person who knows the Ten Commandments perfectly knows the entire Scripture."[1] Is it fair to say that most of us are nowhere close?

If not, this sermon series aims to help us dust off the cobwebs from what some learned long ago and provide others the opportunity to learn them for the first time.

Our goal is not merely to say the words. A parrot could do that! Instead, let's consider the commandments in such a way that they become a lamp that lights our way, a mirror that shows us who we are, and a guardrail that prevents some serious collisions.

We start with the first commandment. This is the most important commandment, the key to all the others. It's like the first button on a shirt.

---

1. Luther, *Large Catechism*, 9.

If you get this one wrong, all the rest will be wrong as well. So let's begin with the first button: "You shall have no other gods."

That sounds simple enough, but what does it mean to have a god? Maybe, in your mind's eye, you are picturing a statue, like one of the great, silent Buddhas in Japan, a statue of Ba'al in ancient Canaan, or an image of the many-armed goddess Kali in India. "Ah, I'm safe," you say. "I've kept that one. I don't have any of those at my house!"

But I repeat, what does it mean to have a god? In his Large Catechism Luther answered the question this way: "To whatever you give your heart and entrust your being, that, I say, is really your God."[2] If we accept Luther's definition, it's clear that there are no atheists. Everyone has some kind of "god."

What people "idolize," what they value most, may not be the true God at all. Some of the most common idols in America are folded up in our wallets, or carried in a six-pack, or driven down the highway.

The human heart, John Calvin liked to say, is a relentlessly efficient factory for producing idols.[3] Your heart is. And so is mine. Before you say, "Not my heart," would you care to test yourself? In the Small Catechism Luther provides three words we can use to measure our propensity toward idolatry. He writes, "We should fear, love, and trust in God above all things."[4]

Very well. What do we fear most? A diagnosis of a terminal illness like cancer or Alzheimer's? The opinions and stares of other people? An economic crash that would wipe out our portfolio? If your boss demanded that you do something illegal or unethical, or if he scheduled you for work hours that would not permit worship, would you agree to his demand because you feared losing your job? What you fear most is a pointer to your real god. If you fear something more than God, you have an idol.

It's even more true with the next word: love. What do you love most? If it's hard to answer that, let me refine the question. On what do you spend the bulk of your time or money—your hobby? What gets your best attention—your job? What do you always seem to wind up talking about—your family, politics? Is there some activity that bumps everything else off your schedule—your favorite sport, your phone or computer? For one family I met, the answer was camping trips. Nothing got in the way of those. Not God. Not a relative's need. Nothing.

2. Luther, *Large Catechism*, 13.
3. Peterson, *Unpredictable Plant*, 81.
4. Luther, *Small Catechism*, 11.

The First Commandment – "No Other Gods"

Who or what do you love most? It's a clue about what drives your life, what is God's biggest competitor. If you love something more than God, you're an idolater.

The third word is trust. In whom or in what do you trust? Our coins say "In God we trust," but that's debatable in a nation that spends about $2.5 billion every day on our defense budget. Our lips say, "In God we trust," but when precarious situations arise, our lawyers, doctors, and insurance agents usually hear from us before God does.

Take a look in the mirror just now and ask yourself: "In what am I trusting? Whom do I love? What do I fear?" There are no atheists. People simply have other gods. Are my fear, love, and trust directed toward the true God or something else?

You shall have no other gods. Why not? Because if you do, they will surely fail you in the end. People disappoint us, and they finally die. Money can be stolen, and it cannot buy happiness or guarantee security. Work can pay the bills, but life needs much more than that.

The word "idol" literally means "a nothing." Idolatry leaves you with nothing in the end. There were more than 1.6 million attempted suicides in our country in the year 2022, more than 4000 every day.[5] How many were because what people feared came true, what they loved didn't satisfy, and what they trusted let them down?

The reason we are to have no other gods is because God alone can deliver all he promises. Right now it may not appear to be so. Those who trust God often suffer grief and privation. For the present. They are harassed by the Devil and ridiculed by scoffers. For the time being. Meanwhile those who grab at things and serve themselves seem bathed in power and prestige and enjoy lots of worldly comforts. For a while! But in the end, says Jesus, those who laugh now will mourn and weep, and those who weep now will laugh (Luke 6:25, 21).

In the end, God will deliver his people. By the mercy of Jesus, he will wipe away their tears, forgive their sins, raise them from death, give them eternal life, and show them their trust in him was well placed. No other "god" can do that.

There it stands: you shall have no other gods.

We know what the commandment means. Is it possible to live by it? Years ago, a woman who was greatly agitated about the moral deterioration of the country wrote to her senator: "Please, senator," she concluded, "make

---

5. CDC. *Suicide Prevention*, par. 2.

them obey the Ten Commandments!" The senator, of course, was unable to help.

No one can enable us to keep this first commandment but God himself. He does not wait for us. He takes the initiative. Before giving the Israelites the commandments, God began by telling them this: "I am the Lord your God who brought you out of Egypt, out of the land of slavery" (Ex 20:1).

Before the commands came the gift, the rescue from slavery. "I have set you free," he told them. "If you want to stay free, here is the way to do it." So he gave them his commandments. But he did much more. For the next 40 years, he led them with a pillar of cloud by day and a pillar of fire by night. He provided miraculous food and water from a rock. He delivered them from enemies and finally brought them to Canaan. Starting at Mt. Sinai, the people had more than his commandments. They had God himself. The God who set them free and kept them free.

This morning we stand in spirit at another mountain. Not Sinai, but Calvary. It is our mountain of rescue. On this mountain is the cross of him who died there to give us an exodus from our idolatries and disloyalties, our foolish fears, our shallow loves, our trust in unreliable helpers.

Because he rose and lives, he gives us even more. He gives us himself for our journey through the wilderness or the metropolis. You shall have no other gods, he says. And we will need no others, for we have his presence and his promise: "I am with you always" (Matt 28:20).

Come with us, Lord, until you finally bring us home!

The Second Commandment – "Using God's Name"

THE FIRST COMMANDMENT ADDRESSES our hearts, directing us to fear, love, and trust God above all else. The second now addresses our lips and tongues, instructing us in the proper use of God's name: "You shall not misuse the name of the Lord your God."

The name in focus is God's name. What's it for, and why does it matter? In Shakespeare's play *Romeo and Juliet*, Juliet stands on her balcony asking that very question, wondering how much it matters that she and Romeo are from two very different families, the Montagues and Capulets. Romeo overhears her saying, "What's in a name? That which we call a rose by any other name would smell as sweet."[1] We wonder the same thing. Why does it matter what name we call God, or how we use his name?

At the very least, a name is a handle by which we make connection. It enables our interaction with others. It is the doorway to a relationship. That's why, day in and day out, we are swamped with names. Friends' names and family names fill the contact lists on our phones. Candidates' names are plastered on billboards and mailed in flyers during political campaigns. Business names compete for our attention with everything from business cards to Super Bowl ads. A thirty-second television ad during the 2024 Super Bowl cost $7 million!

Attached to every name is a reputation. Here's our name, the company tells us. Use it and we can do business. We'll both be happy.

A good name is important, not just for a company doing business, but for each one of us. My name is me. Yours is you. If you have my name, you have me at your disposal. If I have yours, I can reach you. I can bless you, yes I can! Or I can curse you and ruin your reputation and throw a wrench into your relationships.

---

1. Shakespeare, *Romeo and Juliet*, 71–72.

It is the same with God and his name. Next to himself, the most precious thing he gives us humans is his name. It is more than a calling card. If we have his name, we have him, for better or for worse.

That's why, very early in the Bible record, he is cautious about revealing it. Only after centuries of forming his own chosen people did he risk giving Moses his name as Moses stood barefoot and trembling before the burning bush at Sinai. When Moses wonders what he should say if the Israelites ask God's name, he replies, "This is what you are to say to the Israelites: I AM has sent me to you" (Exod 3:14). The Hebrew word for I AM is *Yahweh*, the primary name for God, used some 6800 times in the Old Testament. When you read the Old Testament and see the word LORD in all caps, that's the Hebrew name in the text. It means "He who is" or "He who causes things to be, who brings things into existence." It is a meaning-rich, astonishing name like no other.

This God of ours is no distant deity, observing our lives from afar like on old man on a porch swing. No! This is the God who made all things, cares about all things, who creates and acts.

Take this name, he tells Moses, and use it for the right purpose. Use it to tell the Israelites who I am. Use it to forge a relationship with me. Use it in prayer to call on me in the day of trouble. Take this name, God tells us through his Son Jesus. Hallow it. Use it in a holy way to praise and thank me, to ask forgiveness and protection from the Evil One. Protection, yes! Martin Luther wrote in his Large Catechism, "The devil ... has a very strong distaste for the name of God and cannot stay around long where anyone ... calls upon God's name from the heart."[2]

God gave us his name to use. Later at Sinai came the commandment and the warning not to abuse it: "You shall not misuse the name of the LORD your God." Immediately he attached a stern warning, "for the LORD will not hold anyone guiltless who misuses his name" (Exod 20:7).

The warning had its effect. So seriously did the Jews fear misusing the name they chose not to use it at all! Scribes who copied the Old Testament, when writing the name *Yahweh*, substituted the vowels of the word *Adonai* ("Lord") in its place, so that even today when we read through the Bible, we read the word LORD in all caps.

Perhaps we will think the Jews were being unnecessarily careful, or even silly. That is so because we have the opposite problem. The name of God has come to mean less than it should to most of us because we have

---

2. Luther, *Large Catechism*, 24.

The Second Commandment – "Using God's Name"

lost our sense of reverence and fear. Writer A. W. Tozer, who devoted much time to studying the life of the modern church, observed, "We do not fear God anymore. We do not dread Him anymore. He is our buddy and only wants to help us be the best kind of people we can be."[3] Is he only a "buddy" when he could be infinitely more?

We say his name so easily. So carelessly. If confronted, someone might say, "I didn't mean anything by it." How could it be that one uses the name of God and does not mean anything by it? Is "God" a careless expletive? Is his name simply a handy utterance that slips out if I forget my keys, or get cut off in traffic, or hit my thumb with a hummer? Would you say to his face: "I don't mean anything when I use your name, God"?

Isn't that precisely what the commandment forbids, especially in its older English rendering, "You shall not take the name of the Lord … in vain"? "In vain" means "for nothing," "for no purpose."

If even that is repugnant to God, how much more when humans swear "so help me God" in court and then speak lies, or when they pass off their own false teaching as if it came from God? And what shall we say of one who dares to shove God off the throne and takes over the work of judgment, directing God to "damn" whoever or whatever happens to displease him? Misuses of the name of God, Luther summarized, are "the gravest sins that can be outwardly committed"[4] since the name of God is the holiest thing he has entrusted to us.

What about you? How have you used that name this week? Would it be with joy or with shame if you had to give an account to God today?

And what would you do about the misuse of that name if you were God? With a perfect right, he could punish us all and be done with it. Instead, to rescue and restore his holy name, he dispatched his Son to earth, with orders to live and work among us so that this holy name might be known, honored, and used aright again.

Jesus came and shared an intimate name by which we might come and ask pardon: "Father … forgive us." At the Last Supper, in his high priestly prayer, Jesus asked, "Holy Father, protect them by the power of your name" (John 17:11). The very next morning his shed blood washed away the filth of our sins that had been splattered on God's name. Finally, before his ascension, he commanded his disciples to do an astounding thing—to take the holy name of God and place it on us as our very own name! "Make

---

3. Simmons, Rediscovering our Reverence, par. 3.
4. Luther, *Large Catechism*, 21.

disciples," he commanded, "baptizing them in the name of the Father and of the Son and of the Holy Spirit" (Matt 28:19).

His name is now *your* name, bestowed on you in your baptism. The Book of Revelation gives us the vision of the redeemed standing on Mount Zion with the Lamb's name and the Father's name written on their foreheads. That is a powerful reason for using the name with reverence. God has given us his name to wear! Shouldn't that make a difference in the way we speak that name, and how we live day by day? In the catechism, Luther details the right use of God's name this way: "Call upon it in every trouble, pray, praise, and give thanks."[5]

A woman who had recently become a new believer was in the checkout line at the grocery store. It was a scenario that had played out scores of times in her life before. The checker asked the usual question, "So how are you today?" But the answer this time was different. "God has been so good to me!" she beamed. The woman had a new name. God's name. And she used it in a new way—to give thanks and praise for his goodness so that others might be encouraged to do the same.

What a difference your use of that name will make in the grocery store, the barber shop, the office, the classroom, or wherever you happen to be this week. He has given you his name. Take it with you. Honor him as you speak it to others.

---

5. Luther, *Small Catechism*, 12.

The Third Commandment – "A Day for Remembering"

THE FIRST THREE COMMANDMENTS embrace our duties to God. Commandment one voices God's priority. Commandment two concerns God's name. Today commandment three focuses on God's special day. "Remember the Sabbath day to keep it holy."

"Remember," says the commandment. That's because we are forgetters by nature.

It's bad enough that we forget where we put our glasses, purses, and car keys.

What's worse is forgetting other people. We forget their birthdays. We forget to thank them for their help. We forget promises we made them.

Worst of all, we forget the one who gave us all those things and placed those people into our lives. We forget God. He is being forgotten right now by many whose Sunday morning is devoted to sleeping in, camping out, watching football, or recovering from too many Saturday night beers. Even we who wear the name "Christian" find that working and studying and shopping crowds God off the schedule and distracts our minds from him who deserves our full attention.

Because we so easily forget, God furnished us with a reminder to jog our memories: a day called the Sabbath. Week in, week out. Year in, year out. It's a built-in wakeup call to help forgetters like us remember God.

Right up front we should be clear that God is not so concerned about which day we call the Sabbath as he is about what that day is supposed to do for us. Originally the Sabbath was Saturday, the seventh day of every week, recalling that God rested from his work of creation, as our Seventh-Day Adventist neighbors like to remind us. But we read in Acts 20 that the earliest Christians were already in the habit of meeting on Sunday, the first day of the week, because it was on that day our Lord Jesus rose from the dead. Different day, same purpose: a time to rest, remember, and celebrate the mighty work of God.

Since the observing of different days could provoke a serious quarrel, Saint Paul wrote this instruction to the church in Colossae: "Do not let anyone judge you by what you eat or drink, or with regard to a religious festival, a New Moon celebration, or a Sabbath day" (Col 2:16).

Some set aside Saturdays. We have no quarrel with them. We set aside Sundays.

The real issue concerns what this day is to help us remember about God and about the life he wants us to lead. I hold before you three essential things we are being called to remember.

First we are to remember to rest! That's what the Hebrew word *shabbat* literally means. There at Mt. Sinai God made it abundantly clear: "Six days you shall labor and do all your work, but the seventh day is a Sabbath to the Lord your God. On it you shall not do any work" (Exod 20:9–10).

Notwithstanding the forty-hour work week and the leisure industry boom, this is still a necessary word, isn't it? It's a word to the workaholics among us who may take up a second or even a third job, but then work so hard at our recreation that Monday finds us exhausted instead of refreshed because of our breakneck pace. It's a necessary word in a 24/7 culture with no universal down time. Many a doctor echoes the concern of God by saying, "If you don't slow down and get some rest, this pace will kill you!"

The Sabbath was God's way of saying that, like good music, life needs to have a rhythm of work and built-in rest. At some point we must, as individuals and families, say "no" to the pressure to be constantly busy. We adults must not only tell our children how to do that, but model it as well, with time set aside for quiet walks, quiet talks, good books, and some leisurely rose-smelling.

In his Large Catechism Luther points out that there's a connection between "holy day" and "holiday."[1] The Sabbath is, first of all, a kind of regular holiday for resting. Our culture gladly embraces the increasing number of holidays the government has built into our schedules—Memorial Day, Thanksgiving, the Fourth of July, Veterans Day, and more.

But having a holiday is not enough. Most of us cannot rest without getting restless or even bored. Our inability to relax, our compulsive busyness even when work is done, and our incapacity to endure periods of silence

---

1. Luther, *Large Catechism*, 25.

The Third Commandment – "A Day for Remembering"

without turning on the television reveals an emptiness which only God can fill. "Our hearts are restless," wrote Saint Augustine, "until they can find peace in you."[2] More than a holiday, we need a holy day.

That brings us to the second purpose in the Sabbath. Having remembered to rest, we must also remember God's Word. The Jews did that. They not only stopped working. They gathered as families to share stories of God's mighty acts and sing psalms. They did it first in their homes and then, as centuries passed, in the synagogue. We Christians do the same thing when we gather at church as we do today. Sometimes I am asked, "Does this commandment require that I go to church?" Now and then I hear people say it more defiantly: "I can be a Christian without going to church!" The answer is that going to church is not an end in itself, but a means to an end. The core purpose is the hearing of the Word of God.

Luther explained it this way in his Small Catechism: "We should fear and love God so that we do not despise preaching and His Word, but hold it sacred and gladly hear and learn it."[3] Do you? If you aren't hearing it at church, where are you hearing it? When does God address you, feed you, and correct you?

We Christians are eager to come to church because something precious is here. The Gospel of Jesus is preached. Through that Gospel, God works to free us from our enslavement to sin and death, money, and schedule. The Son of Man, Jesus said, is Lord of the Sabbath. He comes on this holy day to give us himself in the written and spoken Word and the holy meal. People who forget this day and the hearing of the Word will finally forget God and leave a large hole in the middle of their lives.

There is even more to this day of remembering. We remember to rest. We remember God's Word. Finally we remember our neighbor's need.

When the writer to the Hebrews warned his readers not to give up meeting together as some were in the habit of doing, he explained the reason this way: "Let us consider how we may spur up one another on to love and good works" (Heb 10:24). That means worship is not simply my personal filling station. I cannot ignore those who gather with me. Those neighbors need a listening ear and a word of encouragement. And there is a wider circle of need. The community of believers prays, not only for each other, but "for all people according to their needs."

---

2. Augustine, *Confessions*, 17.

3. Luther, *Small Catechism*, 12.

Those prayers lead us to act to feed and clothe and support others. In so doing, we become the body of Christ, serving them with his own compassion and joy. The Gospels frequently portray Jesus as willing to break the Sabbath rules of his day in order to help someone in need. "The Sabbath was made for man, not man for the Sabbath" (Mark 2:27) was Jesus' own explanation. All of that is wrapped up in the Sabbath day, our day for remembering.

The Good News underneath all of it is that God remembers us. He sent his Son Jesus to set us free from our restlessness, from our lovelessness, and yes, even from our forgetfulness.

The Sabbath God gave long ago was a shadow of the things that were to come. The substance belongs to Jesus, whose promise to us exhausted workaholics is "Come to me, all you who are weary and burdened, and I will give you rest" (Matt 11:28).

He himself is our Sabbath rest. Today's the day to lay on him the sin burdens. Today's the day to drop our bundle of worries at his feet. Today's the day for all us absent-minded folks to hear him call us together for a holy holiday that propels us to bless other forgetful people.

One young woman who had finally returned to her faith and her childhood worship habit told her pastor with a big smile, "I can hardly wait until Sunday comes. It's the best day of the week!" Indeed it is.

For her, for us, and for everyone who knows the love of the Savior Jesus, this commandment is not a burden, but a blessing, a foretaste of the feast to come.

The Fourth Commandment – "Honor Your Parents"

THE FIRST THREE COMMANDMENTS embrace our duties to God. Now come seven that tell us our duties to the neighbor. The very first neighbors we meet when we arrive in this world are our parents—dad and mom. The fourth commandment begins with them: "Honor your father and mother."

More than one writer has observed that the hardest place to be a Christian is at home. Do you agree? Home is where the masks come off, and the truth comes out. Home is where sin is most obvious, and grace a daily necessity. Love and respect for other people are learned at home, so God directs us: "Honor your father and mother."

There has been a frightful erosion of respect in our society, whether it is respect for older people, or respect for the authority of parents, teachers, the government, or the church. Pastors often hear heart-wrenching stories about lonely elderly folks abandoned or abused by their own children and of parents whose children use them only as human vending machines. One father lamented, "The only way I know she's still alive and carries my name is because of the bills I get on her credit cards."

It is not a new problem. Sin has eroded relationships and respect from the start, and the family has always been a primary target. Already in Bible times there was disrespect and open rebellion. Remember the sons of Eli? David's troubles with Absalom?

Which of us sitting here doesn't carry some memories of our own disrespect? Didn't we join in the griping when dad or mom told us to make our beds before we went out to play? Didn't we chafe about dating rules and curfews, and didn't we sometimes badmouth our parents in front of our friends? Even now in adulthood, some of us still vent open resentment toward our parents over how to raise our children or spend our vacations. The commandment deserves another look by each of us.

Why is it that God commands us to honor our parents? The Bible lists two obvious reasons. The first is that honoring them comes with the promise of a longer life. God promises it explicitly in Ephesians 6:2–3: "Honor your father and mother . . . that it may go well with you and that you may enjoy long life on the earth."

It isn't hard to see the truth in that. Mother tells her son not to run into the street or play with matches. We can all imagine what will happen if he disobeys. Parents have something that children don't—experience, a wisdom about life that children can't appreciate until later. There's a story that fourteen-year-old Mark Twain said his father was unbearably stupid, but by the time he was twenty-one he was amazed at how much his father had learned in seven years. The story is probably a fabrication, but the point it makes is true enough. As we get older we come to realize our parents knew more than we thought!

There's a second, more basic reason for honoring our parents which has nothing to do with their goodness or wisdom. We are commanded to honor them because they represent God to us. So the first word in this commandment is honor. To honor someone is a weightier matter than to love them. Luther remarked that honoring means realizing that the person honored has a "hidden majesty" because he or she holds an office.[1]

Some people hold a political office, such as a mayor or president. Some people hold a church office, such as a pastor or elder. Mothers and fathers hold the office of parent. They don't wear uniforms or carry badges, but they have a hidden majesty because they represent God to their children. The way you treat them is the way you treat him. Since their office has nothing to do with their intelligence or goodness, one must give them honor at all times, even when they are weak or ill-tempered or unfair.

What we say about honoring parents applies in a derived sense to people who hold other positions of authority. We are, for example, to respect the coach of our team, even if he's a dunce with X's and O's, the boss at work, even if he's foul-mouthed and short on compliments, and the governing authorities, even if they are power-hungry and corrupt.

Before David became Israel's king, he was a servant in King Saul's court and a soldier in Saul's army. His success aroused Saul's envy, which led Saul to pursue David and try to kill him. During those harrowing times, David refused to lift his hand to kill Saul, even when he had the chance.

---

1. Luther, *Large Catechism*, 29.

The Fourth Commandment – "Honor Your Parents"

He explained to his men that he dared not lift a hand against "the Lord's anointed" (1 Sam 24:6).

Luther summed up our duty this way in the Small Catechism: "We should fear and love God so that we do not despise or anger our parents and other authorities, but honor them, serve and obey them."[2]

In keeping with the commandment, we are to pray for those in authority, even if we disagree. If they are in the wrong, we are not to employ violence but seek redress through the law or others in authority to whom we may appeal. If they direct us to disobey the express will of God, we must take the path of civil disobedience, as did the Apostles, who told the Sanhedrin, "We must obey God rather than men" (Acts 5:29).

Honoring the authorities is a very tall order for the child whose parents come home drunk and abusive, the student whose teacher belittles him in front of the class, and citizens whose leaders are incompetent or dishonest.

To stay civil, respectful, and prayerful at such times will be more than we *can* do, or even *want* to do, unless we come at this commandment the way we come at all the others—through Jesus Christ.

Want to keep the fourth commandment? Then remember Jesus. Not the *man* Jesus, first of all, but the *boy*. Remember the twelve-year-old sitting in the Temple asking questions of the elders. Remember the scene in Luke's Gospel? Just when things were getting interesting, in burst his parents. "Son, why have you treated us like this? Your father and I have been anxiously searching for you." His soft brown eyes looked at his mother with love and respect. "Didn't you know I had to be in my Father's house?" (Luke 2:48–49). And that was all. The next moment he put his hand in theirs and went home with them.

The Bible tells us that he went down to Nazareth with them and was obedient to them. For the next eighteen years, little was heard from that lad in Nazareth. What was Jesus doing for all those "silent years"? Practicing miracles? Preparing sermons? No, something more foundational. He was obeying his parents, attending synagogue with them each Sabbath, and learning the carpenter's trade from Joseph. Do those seem small things? Was it unworthy that the Lord of heaven and earth should honor and obey a lowly pair of Jewish peasants?

That obedience was part of what he came to accomplish. He honored and obeyed his earthly parents. Later, in Gethsemane, he honored and

---

2. Luther, *Small Catechism*, 12.

obeyed his heavenly Father. All of it was for us, the offering of his obedience in place of our disobedience, so that when the cross loomed before him, he was ready for it.

What we cannot do, he has done perfectly, and now offers it to us. His obedience to God for our disobedience. His honoring of God for our dishonoring. He offers forgiveness for all the sins that have fractured our families. Take another look at your parents and your children. Between anguished parents and rebellious children, between cruel parents and battered children comes his cross, calling us to peace.

Come, then. Accept his pardon. Share it. Then learn again to honor and respect each other. For in so doing, we shall be honoring him.

The Fifth Commandment – "The Gift of Life"

THE SECOND TABLE OF the Ten Commandments lists our duties to the neighbor. Each one is designed to protect something that belongs to the neighbor. But before we safeguard those things that belong to him, we must first have a neighbor! The fifth commandment protects the neighbor himself, his very life. It is simple and to the point: "You shall not murder."

Years ago when I first learned this commandment, it read "thou shalt not kill." That set off a string of questions in my child's mind. What about soldiers in war? What about policemen shooting criminals? What about butchering animals or even swatting flies? The word "kill" is too general, too ambiguous. What's more, it is not an accurate translation. The original Hebrew word is not *harag*, the general word for "kill," but *ratzah*, which very pointedly means "murder."

You shall not murder. The outward violation of this commandment provides our most shocking headlines. Terrorist Attack on the World Trade Center! Gunman Massacres School Children in Newtown, Connecticut! Serial Killer Strikes Again!

Murder is condemned by every culture on earth. Everyone agrees about this commandment. Accordingly, it appears to be the easiest of the ten to keep. Yes, we might say, murder is shocking, but it is rare. Am I safe in guessing that no one here in church today has planted a bomb? Stabbed a neighbor to death? Shot someone in cold blood? It would be easy to breathe a sigh of relief and say, "No murderers here in church today" and move on to the next commandment.

But God says, "Not so fast." Take a closer look at your life and at this deceptively simple commandment. For it may be broken in at least four different ways. The first three are by my hand, by my tongue, and in my heart.

With my hand, I may hold a gun and pull a trigger. But hands do other things. With his hand, a doctor may insert a metal instrument into a pregnant uterus to kill an unborn child. With his hand, a man may open a bottle of pills to swallow and end his own life. With the hands a parent may beat a child bloody and senseless. In your hand you may hold a cigarette with its small dose of a lethal, addictive poison called nicotine. There are many ways to kill with one's hands. Some are slow, some fast. Some are quiet and hidden. Many could be called "murder."

But Jesus made clear that the tongue may also be used to murder the neighbor. The tongue is only a few ounces of flesh, but it may be sharper than a dagger. You've heard of "back-stabbing"? That isn't done by one's hand. It's a murder by the tongue. "The tongue is a fire . . ." wrote James, "a restless evil, full of deadly poison" (Jas 3:6, 8).

Years ago as a young boy I heard a sermon on the warning Jesus made in the Sermon on the Mount: "Anyone who says, 'You fool!' will be in danger of the fire of hell" (Matt 5:22). Later that very afternoon I quarreled with my younger brother and called him names. One of them was "fool." In mid-sentence I stopped, remembering the dreadful warning of that sermon. How about your tongue? Has it dished out any little murders lately?

No? Then go deeper. Into your heart, where things happen in secret, things heard and seen by God alone. There, deep down, in every one of us, lurks the hatred and the settled instinct for revenge that paces around like a caged animal. Imagine that you are in some infuriating situation with someone who persistently irks you. If you were in a cartoon, the bubble over your head might read: "The urge to kill."

That urge lives inside each of us, quiet and camouflaged. Sometimes it erupts. In December of 1984, Bernard Goetz, a thin man with glasses, had been hassled and threatened once too often by some teenagers on a Manhattan subway train. He drew a gun and shot four of them. Lots of people cheered. Goetz became a hero and got a nickname: "The Subway Vigilante."

Such a reaction to the story reveals us for what we are—a people prone to violence. Potential and actual murderers. We kill with our hands, our tongues, and our hearts. Those are three well-known ways to break this commandment.

But there is a fourth, also deadly. It is to do nothing for the neighbor when we could (and should) do something. Call it the Cain Complex. It asks, "Am I my brother's keeper?" (Gen 4:9). It's looking the other way, passing by the fallen victims on life's Jericho Road and saying, "I wouldn't hurt a fly" or "I mind my own business," as did the priest and the Levite in Jesus' story of the Good Samaritan.

The Fifth Commandment – "The Gift of Life"

In this commandment, as in all of them, there is not only a wrong God forbids but a right he commands. Stated positively, the fifth commandment is a call to seek the neighbor's physical welfare. Not merely "Live and *let* live," but "Live and *help* live." Luther summed it up this way in his Small Catechism: "We should fear and love God so that we do not hurt or harm our neighbor in his body, but help and support him in every physical need."[1] Very simply, God commands us to help our neighbor.

But who *are* my neighbors? The people next door? All my acquaintances? Surely, we owe such people our love and care. Even unbelievers know that. And even unbelievers can do that. Jesus urges us to go further and show loving care to strangers. The man on the Jericho road was finally helped by a total stranger. That man's kindness has given a name to strangers who stop by to do that on the highways and byways of our lives. We call them "Good Samaritans."

But God's intent goes even further. Not only friends. Not only strangers. But even enemies are to receive loving care. How is that possible?

How, wondered Joyce, a junior high student who was belittled day after day by her science teacher in front of the class. "How can I love him?" she cried to her parents after an especially painful day.

By herself, Joyce could not. By ourselves, we cannot. But we are not by ourselves. Beside us stands the one who said, "Love your enemies." Jesus said it. Then he did it. When he was accused and mocked, he did not retaliate. When he was crucified, he prayed for his killers, "Father, forgive them, for they do not know what they are doing" (Luke 23:34). He said it about the soldiers who nailed him there. He said it about us, whose murderous, hurtful sins put him there. "Father, forgive them."

Jesus looks at us with eyes that made us and love us still. If we are to keep this commandment, we will need to look at life through his eyes, and see life as a gift that God alone can give and God alone can take away. Through his eyes we see our neighbors as people for whom Jesus came, for whom he lived and died and rose.

That's what Joyce's mother told her. "I know this teacher has hurt you," she said. "But try to see him as someone for whom Jesus died. How do you think Jesus would treat him?" Joyce thought about it. The next day was the same as before. But Joyce was different. When the bell rang, Joyce stopped at her teacher's desk and deposited a package. Then, without a word, she

---

1. Luther, *Small Catechism*, 12.

left. When the teacher opened the box, he saw some cookies, and this note: "God loves you, and I'll try too."

Do you want to love that hard-to-love neighbor? Would you like to bury the hatchet and start over again? Then start with yourself, and know that God in Christ has loved you. He gave you life as a gift. For the sins and hurts, he holds out complete pardon. He went to the cross for you.

Then look again at the neighbor. Remember the cross, and ask the Lord to let you see with his eyes. When you do, you will know how to live and help live.

The Sixth Commandment – "In Matters of Sex"

IN THIS SERIES ON the Ten Commandments, we have made our way to number six: "You shall not commit adultery."

If someone conducted a Ten Commandments popularity poll, this one would probably finish last. No other commandment has gotten such a bad reputation. God is, some complain, a celestial spoilsport who throws a wet blanket over the fun they want to have. Christians are labeled prudes, accused of being obsessed with policing people's private lives and saying "No" to most everything connected with sex.

To be sure, there is a "you shall not" in this commandment. But that's not all there is to it. God says no to adultery, no to sex outside of marriage, no to pornography, because he wants to say a bigger yes to the love and companionship he has in mind for us inside marriage. God says no to the abuse and misuse of this gift so that it might be the bountiful blessing he intended, not a problem.

But it has become a problem, hasn't it? It isn't just the church saying so. The Pan American Health Organization has identified more than thirty different sexually-transmitted infections[1] that affect one in five Americans and lead to sterility, cancers, and death, as well as costing $16 billion per year in treatment costs.[2] Does that have your attention?

There's more. Social agencies have anguished over the fact that 40 percent of all children born in the USA are born out of wedlock.[3] The odds that those children will have problems with poverty, crime and unhappy homes are staggeringly high.[4] Community leaders, town councils, and law enforcement officials wrestle with a floodtide of pornography on the

---

1. *Sexually Transmitted Infections,* PAHO, par. 1.
2. *Sexually Transmitted Infections,* CDC, par. 1.
3. Wildsmith, *Dramatic Increases,* par. 1.
4. Marripedia, *Effects of Out-of-Wedlock Births,* pars 1–3.

internet and worry about its dehumanizing effect, especially on women. There's no need to define pornography, is there? In 1964 Supreme Court Justice Potter Stewart, weighing in on the obscenity of a current film, famously said, "I know it when I see it."[5]

Where is our society headed? It seems more and more like a car careening out of control, going the wrong direction on a busy freeway. Deadly collisions are inevitable. Many pastors observe that more permanent and utter devastation is done in matters of sexual behavior than in any other area because it is so personal, so powerful. We all know people with shattered dreams and devastated families.

Luther saw it already long ago. In commenting specifically about the impact of adultery on one's neighbor, he wrote in his Large Catechism, "There is no possession of his [more than his spouse] through which greater injury could be done to him."[6]

Just what *is* the problem with sex? For a long time, people thought the problem was silence. Keeping things "hush-hush." The church was accused of joining the conspiracy of silence. How things have changed since our grandparents' day! Now people talk openly and endlessly about it. We are overwhelmed. Deluged. We live in a sex-saturated society. And still the problems persist.

The problem isn't silence. The problem certainly isn't sex itself. One cannot blame a car for careening down the highway. The fault lies with the driver. The problem isn't sex. It's sin. The commandment reveals us for what we are—an adulterous and sinful generation. Therefore God speaks this word to our society and us personally: "You shall not commit adultery."

What does the commandment mean? To "adulterate" means to pollute—to add something impure. Years ago the Cuyahoga River in Cleveland became so polluted that it actually caught on fire. To apply that picture, God designed sex to be a beautiful river of life and blessing. One might think of marriage as the joining of two separate healthy streams into one. Don't pollute it, says God. Don't pollute it with your mouth by telling filthy jokes and suggestive stories. Don't pollute it with your eyes by watching pornographic videos. If that sounds like a big helping of "don't," remember that this commandment has a flip side. Do be faithful. Do stay pure. Do enjoy sex as a part of a committed and loving marriage in which you give all of yourself and not just a small part.

---

5. Washington University, *I Know it When I See it*, par. 1.
6. Luther, *Large Catechism*, 44.

The Sixth Commandment – "In Matters of Sex"

In his Small Catechism, Luther stressed the positive: "We should fear and love God so that we lead a sexually pure and decent life in what we say and do, and husband and wife love and honor each other."[7]

What's the purpose of this word? At a church meeting one night came this question: "What do you think of the Ten Commandments?" Among a variety of replies came this thoughtful response from one woman: "God must have loved us very much to give them to us, to protect us from ourselves." Hear this commandment, first, as a protecting word. Like the signs that say "Speed Limit 55," designed with your safety in mind, so this commandment is designed to protect you—your marriage, your family, and even your life.

To whom is it addressed? It seems, at first glance, that it speaks only to married people. But Luther goes on to point out that in Old Testament times, marriage was obligatory among the Jews, and that many were married very early so that sexual sin was almost always in the category of adultery.[8]

The Bible makes clear, however, that God's protective umbrella is wider and applies to all people, married or unmarried. Our Lord's warning against lust included anyone who looks on a woman to lust after her. Saint Paul, an unmarried man, laid down guidelines for both married people and single people.

Are you married? Hear this as God's urging to cherish the spouse he gave you. If you have married children, encourage them to remain loyal and work through their conflicts with God's help. Too many parents offer an escape hatch by saying, "Any time you want, you can come home!"

Are you single? Not yet married? No matter. God speaks to you here as well. Have a high view of marriage. Don't let the failures of others disillusion you. There are good marriages, and with God's help you can have one. If you stay single, stay chaste. Devote yourself to God's service. Save yourself for the husband or wife he may have waiting for you.

That is God's Word to us in this commandment. A good word. A protecting word. Yet by itself it is not enough. Road signs do not make good drivers. They only restrain bad ones. This commandment, by itself, cannot solve the problems we have with sex. It will not change people on the inside.

More than God's word of *command*, we need God's word of *rescue*.

---

7. Luther, *Small Catechism*, 12.
8. Luther, *Large Catechism*, 44.

Long ago God set apart a prophet named Hosea and gave him an astonishing assignment. "Go, take to yourself an adulterous wife and children of unfaithfulness" he commanded (Hos 1:2). Hosea obeyed, married Gomer, and endured the heartache of her unfaithfulness. When Gomer left him, he pursued her, paid money to buy her back, and brought her home.

Hosea's life became a picture, lived out in flesh, of God's relentless love for his unfaithful people Israel. It was a picture that pointed ahead to the coming of Jesus, who became the bridegroom to us all. In him, God relentlessly wooed and pursued all of us adulterers with his cleansing, rescuing love. We sing of it in one of our hymns: "From heaven He came and sought her to be His holy bride. With His own blood He bought her, and for her life He died."

In that hymn and these preached words, hear him saying it to you: "I love you. I have bought you back. Come home!" For it is only in being passionately pursued and faithfully loved by him that we come to know what love is, and that we are empowered to be the chaste and holy husbands and wives he intended us to be.

If you have sinned in matters of sex, bring him that sin today and hear his word of pardon. Jesus came to forgive this too. By his grace, make a new beginning. Pray for his Holy Spirit and that blessed fruit of self-control.

By his grace, you may again enjoy that life he gives you as a gift, free to love, free to serve, free to glorify God in your body.

The Seventh Commandment – "A Parade of Thieves"

I BEGIN THE SERMON today with a Bible trivia question. Ready? What do Jacob and Rachel, Aachan, Zacchaeus, Judas, Barabbas, and Ananias and Sapphira all have in common?

Have you guessed? All of them were thieves. Winding through the Bible, and through the pages of all recorded history, is a long parade of thieves. Some are legendary—like Robin Hood or Bonnie and Clyde. Most remain in the shadows, and some are thieves without even realizing it.

The sobering truth is that you and I are part of this parade too, and addressing us all this morning comes a word from God, the seventh of the Ten Commandments: "You shall not steal."

Do we need to define stealing? Luther's definition in the Large Catechism is that stealing is "nothing other than acquiring someone else's property by unjust means."[1] That includes taking advantage of him in any sort of way that results in his loss.

God forbids it, but people pay little attention. Stealing has become a widespread and very common kind of vice. Luther goes on to observe: "Thievery is . . . the most common craft and the largest trade union on earth. When humankind is analyzed … it turns out to be simply one great, wide warehouse full of superthieves."[2]

Do you think he is exaggerating? If you do, perhaps it is because when you think of "stealing," you picture bank robbers wearing masks, carrying guns, escaping in getaway cars. In reality, there are many other ways to steal.

There is the sort we call petty theft because what is taken is so small. I did it as a child in the grocery store when I nibbled grapes from the produce table. Employees in an office do it when they "borrow" pencils, paper clips, and rubber bands from the supply room to take home, sometimes by the

1. Luther, *Large Catechism*, 47.
2. Luther, *Large Catechism*, 49.

boxful! It sounds petty unless you are the store owner or company manager who has to cover the cost of all the missing supplies.

Another form of stealing is dishonest trading. Selling shoddy merchandise. Overcharging your customers. What about the car dealer who sells you a "lemon"? Or the mechanic who charges you to fix something that wasn't broken? I'm remembering a landlord in St. Louis who refused to return our deposit when we moved out because, he alleged, the apartment wasn't clean enough, even though we had cleaned it thoroughly.

And shall we not mention a particularly common sort of theft called laziness on the job? Employees come in a bit late, and leave a bit early. Coffee breaks and lunch hours stretch a few minutes longer. Workers find ways to be shirkers and thereby deprive the company of a full day's work, though they get a full day's pay. But who will dare confront them and call them thieves?

Thievery takes so many forms that we practically run out of words. I haven't yet mentioned pickpockets and extortioners, embezzlers and counterfeiters, identity thieves and con artists, shoplifters and writers of bad checks.

Stealing, of course, doesn't always involve money or goods. A student cheating on a test at school is stealing answers. A plagiarist steals someone's ideas and presents them as his own. On a larger scale, many American corporations steal trade secrets and technology from one another. One cultural observer put it simply: "Everybody steals from everybody."

At some point or other, "everybody" includes you and me. Each of us has joined the parade of thieves. Every time we see a lock on a door, it is an indictment of the kind of world we live in and the sort of people we all are.

God isn't joking when he says, "You shall not steal." He forbids it for two good reasons. First, because stealing hurts the neighbor. If you have been robbed, you know from personal experience how it feels like a blow to the stomach, especially if the thief takes something irreplaceable.

There is a second reason God forbids stealing. That is because the thief is shoving God aside. The Psalmist says "The earth is the Lord's" (Ps 24:1). But the thief says, "No. It is not yours, God; it is mine. I defy your wisdom. I disagree with your policy of distribution. I hereby take matters into my own hands!"

God says "Love your neighbor as yourself" (Matt 22:39). The thief says, "No. I love myself, and I will use my neighbor to get what I want!"

The Seventh Commandment – "A Parade of Thieves"

With such words on our lips and thoughts in our hearts, we join the parade of thieves.

But God does not sit idly by and endure such rebellion. The police may not be able to collar every thief, but in the end, none will escape the judgment of God. "The wicked," wrote St. Paul, "will not inherit the kingdom of God . . . nor thieves, nor the greedy . . . And that is what some of you were" (1 Cor 6:9, 10, 11).

Now and then in the Bible, God's judgment falls suddenly upon thieves. Aachan and his family had stolen devoted items from Jericho and hidden them in their tent, but God found them out, and he and his family were stoned to death. Ananias and Sapphira lied about a donation to the poor and held back a part for themselves. God struck them dead at Peter's feet, and the Book of Acts tells us that great fear seized the whole church.

Yet God's purpose in this commandment is not to frighten us, but to teach us how to live together peaceably. Not to destroy us but to change us. Otherwise, if every thief were caught and executed, the world would soon be empty.

God intends to halt this parade of thieves and turn the heart of each one. Paul spells it out plainly in Ephesians 4:28: "He who has been stealing must steal no longer, but must work, doing something useful with his own hands, that he may have something to share with those in need."

That very transformation happened to a little man named Zacchaeus. Though small in stature, he was a big-time thief who ripped off citizens by collecting more taxes than was lawful. But his story ended happily, for one day he met a man who changed him. Jesus spied Zacchaeus in a tree, loved him, and said, "Zacchaeus, come down immediately. I must stay at your house today" (Luke 19:5).

Jesus never condoned stealing. He made that clear when he drove the money-changers from the Temple, calling them robbers. But though he hated sins against this commandment, he loved the thieves themselves. He meets this parade of thieves and pulls first one then another out. Judas he brought into the circle of disciples. Barabbas he set free and took his place on the cross. He died in the place of one thief and between two others!

In truth, it was not just for Barabbas he died, but for every thief, including *us*. He did it to give us a lasting treasure in heaven. He became poor to make us rich in a way that lasts into eternity!

But he did it for another reason as well—to show us how to live until we get there. Zacchaeus understood at once. The same day Jesus came into his home, he made changes. The people he had defrauded he repaid fourfold. And with the rest of his money he became a generous giver.

The Small Catechism sums up the commandment thus: "We should fear and love God so that we do not take our neighbor's money or possessions, or get them in any dishonest way, but help him to improve and protect his possessions and income."[3]

That's why we gather an offering each Sunday. It is not an *intermission* from worship but an integral *act* of worship. It is loving our neighbor in a tangible way.

This morning, the parade of thieves winds to the cross where thieves are pardoned and changed and life begins anew.

Let us lay our burdens down here, accept that pardon gratefully, and learn from him to share with our neighbor what he entrusted to us.

---

3. Luther, *Small Catechism*, 13.

The Eighth Commandment – "My Neighbor's Good Name"

ONCE UPON A TIME there was a certain King Alfred who ruled his country from a sumptuous castle. He was rich, but unhappy, for one of his subjects had spread lies about him and ruined his reputation. Distraught, he sent this message to his accuser: "Take my castle, my horse, and my armor. All these I'd gladly yield if only you would give me back my old good name."

Everyone has a name. But not everyone has a good name, that is, a good reputation. Poor King Alfred discovered that a good name is priceless. Once lost, it is very hard to get it back. Consider the grade school boy who gets the label "troublemaker." That reputation may follow him for years, for a lifetime!

How about you? What's your reputation in this community, this congregation? This morning I invite you to think about names. Your own. And your neighbor's.

God makes it clear that he intends to protect that neighbor's name. He will have no one deprived of his honor and reputation. Therefore he erects a wall around that neighbor's name with the words of the eighth commandment. Say it with me: "You shall not bear false witness against your neighbor."

At its simplest level, this commandment refers to the courtroom and those who take the witness stand. Here we must speak truth about the neighbor or careers will be ruined, and lives may be lost.

The Bible tells the story of a good man named Naboth, a simple farmer who refused to sell his vineyard to King Ahab. Ahab was frustrated by the refusal and sulked. It was left to Queen Jezebel to devise a solution. She hired false witnesses to lie about Naboth in court. Their lies prevailed. Innocent Naboth was executed, and his vineyard was stolen thereafter by Ahab (1 Kings 21:1–16).

Such things happen today with disturbing frequency, in spite of laws against perjury. All of us have heard stories of people finally released after years of imprisonment for crimes they never committed!

You say you've never been in a courtroom? No matter. There's a wider sense in which this commandment touches all of us. For day after day we are talking about other people. Students talk about their teachers. In the next room, teachers are comparing notes about those students! Workers talk about their supervisors, and each other. Neighbors pass news about neighbors to other neighbors.

It's no different here at church, is it? Listen in our hallways, in the kitchen, in the parking lot. Every church (including ours) has a "grapevine" along which we pass information about other people.

In this commandment, God pulls us up short and asks, "What are you saying about others?" There are at least three tests to make on what we say about other people. Is it true? Is it necessary? And is it loving?

First, is it true? If this sounds obvious, ask yourself how often you must filter what you read or see in the media. When I was young, I trusted much of what I read in the newspaper and what I heard from Walter Cronkite or Peter Jennings on television. No longer! Now I suspect "media bias" almost everywhere. You too? Fact-checkers abound, and they hand out ratings: "One Pinocchio!" "Three Pinocchios!" "Pants on fire!"

But the sad truth is that even the fact-checkers can't always be trusted. We long for truth in our media. Should we expect less of ourselves? A spoken lie that ruins a reputation is called slander, a vicious sin that God condemns: "You speak continually against your brother and slander your own mother's son . . . I will rebuke you and accuse you to your face" (Ps 50:20–21).

Besides asking "Is it true?" we must ask further, "Is it necessary?" It is necessary that witnesses in court speak out for the sake of justice. It is necessary that parents discuss their children and that teachers inform parents for the sake of education. It is necessary for the sake of godliness that pastors admonish the congregation's members who stray.

But how necessary is it that you speak about person A to person B? Is it, as Ephesians 4 says, helpful for building others up? Does it benefit those who listen? How often have we had to say, with tears, "I wish I'd kept my mouth shut!"?

Third, is it loving? Ephesians 4 goes on to direct that we are to be "speaking the truth in love" (Eph 4:15). For even the truth should not always be spoken! How would you feel if, starting tomorrow, someone who knows you well began telling everyone every true thing about you, including every mean or careless thing you had told him? And how would you react if, when you confronted this mouthy person, he or she said, "Oh, don't worry, I won't say anything that isn't true"?

There are words for such people. As children we called them tattletales. As adults we call them gossips. Sadly, for every gossip there are many eager ears waiting to hear the worst about others. Luther compared such people to pigs: "When they have heard some tidbit, they carry it to every corner . . . delighting in roiling up someone else's dirt like pigs that wallow in the muck and root around in it with their snouts."[1]

Why do we love to hear the worst about others? Because gossiping has a payoff. We trade small talk about others for power, fun, information, and even money. Call it using others for our own ends. More pointedly, call it alienation and hatred for the neighbor.

God arrests us with the commandment: "You shall not bear false witness against your neighbor." To say it positively: love your neighbor. Love him enough to protect his name. Love him enough, says the catechism, to "defend him, speak well of him, and explain his actions in the kindest way."[2]

How do you fare under the probing searchlight of this commandment? How many of us sitting here in church must stand shame-faced before God this morning and confess that we are gossips and slanderers, back-stabbers and rumor-mongers, and that our "grapevines" are often growing sour grapes?

If it is your besetting sin to damage your neighbor's name, bring it to God. He is in the business of cleaning filthy mouths, bridling careless tongues, and restoring damaged names. Ask Isaiah, the man of unclean lips whose mouth was touched by God (Isa 6:5–7). Ask Saul the Persecutor, whose name was changed to Paul the Apostle and whose mouth was filled with a different message (Acts 9:1–22).

God dispatched his Son Jesus to set things right. Part of his mission was to bear on his shoulders the vicious and venomous sins of our mouths. He did this literally. Remember how they called him names? "Glutton" and "drunkard," "a man born of fornication," they jeered. "He has a demon," they whispered on their grapevine. While he rode meekly into Jerusalem on that donkey, his enemies were plotting murder against him.

---

1. Luther, *Large Catechism*, 55.
2. Luther, *Small Catechism*, 13.

What happened to Naboth happened to him. A parade of false witnesses came to spout their lying nonsense. Then, amid taunts and curses, he was executed for our lies, for our gossip, for our venomous tongues.

When at last he rose on Easter, God bestowed on him "the name that is above every name, that at the name of Jesus every knee should bow and every tongue . . ." (Phil 2:9–10). And every tongue do what?

If Jesus died to forgive my tongue, shall my tongue not show it?

Let me hold before you three ways our tongues may show their Master to be Jesus and their ministry love.

First, by *keeping silent* much more often. In his book *Life Together* Dietrich Bonhoeffer called it "the ministry of holding one's tongue," in which each individual, including pastors, would refrain from saying much that occurs to him.[3] It is vital for pastors to keep their mouths shut, for they hear much that is meant to be private and that would be very damaging to utter. Luther directs all of us in his catechism, "Let your ear become (a) grave."[4]

Second, by *praying* before we speak. Does someone irk you? Repulse you? Then place that person in your daily prayers before you speak, or you will surely say the wrong things.

Third, if the brother or sister sins against you, *speak privately* to them, or else say nothing at all. "If your brother sins against you," said Jesus, "go and show him his fault just between the two of you" (Matt 18:15).

All of this is essential because the neighbor is a gift to us from God. That neighbor's name is his priceless possession. Pray for him. Speak well of him. Encourage him. For in him we meet Christ himself.

---

3. Bonhoeffer, *Life Together*, 91–2.
4. Luther, *Large Catechism*, 55.

The Ninth and Tenth Commandments – "No Coveting!"

TODAY WE CONCLUDE OUR series on the Ten Commandments. The last two begin with the same words, so we consider them together. They are written on your bulletin. Will you recite them with me? "You shall not covet your neighbor's house. You shall not covet your neighbor's wife, or his manservant or His maidservant, his ox or donkey, or anything that belongs to your neighbor."

Those words were etched in stone on a mountain centuries ago. Are they still relevant today? Let's switch scenes to a location nearby in time and place. Sit down in a television studio. Look and listen to what unfolds.

Before us a dapper accountant named Kevin adjusts his collar as the hands of the studio clock tick away the final seconds before air time. To his left an airline flight attendant named Eileen hastily checks her makeup with a pocket mirror.

Suddenly the red light flashes, and the show is on. The host asks questions. With his first correct answer the accountant wins a microwave oven. He jumps for joy. An incorrect answer costs the flight attendant a solid oak dining room set, and her distress is palpable. More questions. Some good answers by both. The audience claps. Finally, as the last seconds of the program tick away, the genial host of "What's My Loot?" tabulates the winnings Kevin and Eileen have amassed, accompanied by plenty of "oohs" and "ahs" from the audience. Meanwhile, out in TV land, thousands of viewers sigh enviously: "Why couldn't that have been me?"

Perhaps, some day, it will be. Isn't that part of the American dream? Wealth. Financial security. The vision of prosperity grabs people. It stokes the fire of our ambitions. "You can have it all!" That's the theme song of most commercials, the drumbeat that drives our way of life.

But that hunger, that desire to have it all brings us smack up against these last two commandments: "You shall not covet." Coveting means wanting, yearning to possess, persistently craving more and more things, in particular the things my neighbor has, until those things occupy the center of my life.

Maybe you're convinced, as many are, that all this isn't such a big deal, really. After all, everybody wants good things. Who wouldn't mind getting rich? Or at least financially comfortable? So people flock to play bingo in church basements and stand in line for a couple of lottery tickets every week. Everybody wants stuff, don't they? And who am I hurting if I take on another job or work some overtime every week? At least I'm not stealing!

If coveting's a sin, it's surely a minimum sin, hardly to be mentioned with the big-time wickedness the other eight commandments condemn. Nothing to get upset about. No reason for a sermon to pick on game shows and lottery tickets. C'mon, preacher, hit the sex and violence, the robbery and fraud, the perjury on the witness stand, and phony preachers who peddle man-made doctrines as God's own truth.

These two commandments seem to deserve their place in the Decalogue—last and least!

We think so, that is, until we begin to listen seriously to what the Bible says about coveting, also translated as "greed." Like these words in Ephesians 5:5: "No . . . greedy person . . . has any inheritance in the kingdom of Christ and of God." Or these in Colossians 3:5: "Put to death, therefore, whatever belongs to your earthly nature . . . and greed, which is idolatry."

Martin Luther says, surprisingly, that these last two commandments are "not addressed to those whom the world considers scoundrels, but precisely to the most respectable,"[1] to people who are industrious and ambitious, who may work hard for a living. They are a warning that says, "Look out! Coveting may lead you away from God."

Coveting brought a sad ending to the story of the rich, young ruler who came to Jesus seeking eternal life. He had kept all the other commandments, he said, but he never mentioned coveting. In the end, the love of things led him away from Jesus and life.

Or how about the sobering story Jesus told about the rich farmer who planned to build bigger barns for all his "stuff," until the fateful night God said, "You fool! This very night your life will be demanded from you. Then who will get what you have prepared for yourself?" (Luke 12:20). The

---

1. Luther, *Large Catechism*, 60.

The Ninth and Tenth Commandments – "No Coveting!"

farmer was a smart man who liked to plan ahead. The problem was that his pursuit of his dream of wealth left him with no time for God.

That's the problem with all coveting. It fixes our minds on things and entices our hearts away from God. These two commandments address not our *outward behavior* but our *hearts*. Offenses against them are not obvious, for the coveter may appear technically law-abiding.

The covetous man makes someone else's worker an offer he can't refuse and pries him away from that company. Acquaintances commend him for his "boldness." He makes crafty legal maneuvers by which he tricks his gullible relatives out of their inheritance, and observers call him "shrewd." A law-abiding schemer he is, continues Luther, who "slyly loosens something from another's grasp," who "pressures his victim until he has taken over half of his property or more."[2]

Outwardly we can see no law being broken, but God sees the real drama unfolding in the heart. So it is that by the last two commandments God would fence the heart. For it is out of the heart, said Jesus, that proceed all the other sins—evil thoughts, murder, adultery, sexual immorality, theft, false testimony, slander. Coveting, which you *cannot* see, gives rise to all those other spectacular sins which you *can*.

Consider two people in particular whose coveting led to dreadful sins. David coveted Uriah's wife, and that coveting led to adultery and then murder (2 Sam 11). Judas coveted those 30 pieces of silver, and his coveting led to the betrayal and death of Jesus, then finally to Judas's own suicide (Matt 26:14–16; Acts 1:18–19). Like a weed in your garden, coveting starts small, but grows and grows until it takes over your life.

In Leo Tolstoy's story *How Much Land Does a Man Need?* the hero is told he can have all the land around which he can plow a furrow in a single day. The excited man starts vigorously and by midday has a nice plot. But fully half a day remains and he sees he can get much more, so he continues to plow feverishly, and as the sun goes down he fairly races to get back to his point of departure. But the effort proves too much. As he struggles toward the finish, he gasps and falls, the victim of a heart attack! For his day's work, he inherits a burial plot.

Could that be you? Or me? Are we plowing through life as hard as we can to get as much as we can, congratulating ourselves that we are, in fact, decent folks who haven't committed murder or adultery, who haven't robbed a bank and don't use curse words? It is just when we think such

---

2. Luther, *Large Catechism*, 61.

things in our smug complacency that these final two commandments arrest us and expose us for what we really are— covetous rebels who love ourselves more than God or the neighbor.

So where are we to find help?

Certainly not from these two commandments, nor from the other eight. From the law we get only a jolt meant to lead us to repentance, like the doctor's diagnosis that leads to surgery.

The help our good doctor God provides is through his Son Jesus. The Giver came to rescue the grabbers. His sacrifice on the cross was the vital surgery that lanced our infected hearts, drained the toxin of covetousness, and brought us forgiveness.

But forgiveness is only the beginning of what God has in mind. His long-range plan is to give each of us a heart transplant, to remove the old, clogged, covetous heart and give us a new one, warm with the love of God and our neighbor. The surgeon is the Holy Spirit. His scalpel is the Word of God. His sutures are placed by prayer.

As our hearts heal by his daily care, the Holy Spirit will nourish us with his array of delicious fruits (like joy and peace and self-control) and his great gift of generosity. "Covet these!" he says. Against such there is no law, and the supply is inexhaustible.

By His grace, God supplies all we need. Aren't you glad?

With that, we have come to the end of this series on the Ten Commandments. Would you have more success now listing them from memory? More important, do you have a better understanding of their purpose in your daily life?

The Ten Commandments are like a mirror. Daily we look into them and see that Christ must wash us all over again.

Let him do that for you today and every day. Let them drive you back to the Savior. He will make you clean again and supply you with an abundant life.

The Apostles' Creed

Creed Sermon One – "What Does it Mean to Believe?"

TODAY WE BEGIN A series of sermons on the Apostles' Creed.

May it be for you a real adventure of faith. By the end of this series, I hope you'll be able to say, with greater conviction, "I know what I believe, why I believe it, and how I intend to live because of it."

Why the Apostles' Creed?

There are two good reasons. First, because there's no better summary of the Christian faith. Martin Luther called it "the entire Christian faith in three chief articles."[1] This creed is comprised of three short paragraphs—one about the Father, a second about the Son, the third about the Holy Spirit. The whole creed is little more than one hundred words long. It is brief, yet inclusive. One early church leader praised it for being small in the number of words, but great in the importance of its ideas.

The second reason for preaching on the creed is that it is something on which almost all Christians agree. With all our divisions and disagreements, we lose sight of our underlying unity. Shortly after his conversion in 1929, C. S. Lewis wrote to a friend: "When all is said ... about the divisions of Christendom, there remains, by God's mercy, an enormous common ground."[2]

The Apostles' Creed is one of three so-called ecumenical creeds known and accepted by many different denominations around the world. And not only by those alive today. When we confess this creed, we link arms across the centuries with John Calvin and Martin Luther King, with David Livingstone and Florence Nightingale, with St. Francis of Assisi and King Henry VIII.

---

1. Luther, *Large Catechism*, 68.
2. Lewis, *Christian Reflections*, vii.

Just how old is this creed? The title might lead you to think it was written by the Twelve Apostles themselves. In the early centuries, that's what some people thought. In an earlier form, the Apostles' Creed consisted of twelve statements. The legend arose that on Pentecost Day, each of the Apostles in turn was inspired by the Spirit to stand and contribute a statement, and that the creed was the result.

The fact is, however, that the creed in its present form dates from the sixth or seventh century after Christ, although its roots go back much further. Most of it had been assembled by AD 390. Though it was not written by the Apostles, it surely expresses their teaching and faith—a faith we share with them.

The Apostles' Creed is a statement of faith. The word "creed" comes from the Latin word *credo*, which means "I believe." And those are the very words that begin this creed: "I believe in …" We've said that many times. But just what is faith? What does it mean to believe? Let's complete the sentence "Faith is …" with three different words, each of which builds on the one before. Faith is knowing. Faith is accepting. Faith is trusting. Think about each of those words.

First, faith is *knowing*. If a person says, "I believe," the question that follows automatically is "Believe in *whom*? Believe in *what*?" Years ago there was a lot of talk about UFOs. My wife and I used to have discussions about them. Did I believe in them, or didn't I? I'll pass the question on. Do *you* believe in UFOs? You can't say "Yes, I do" until you know what's meant by "UFO"—Unidentified Flying Object. We used to call them "flying saucers."

In the same way, one cannot believe in Jesus Christ, or the resurrection from the dead, or in God at all, unless he knows what is meant by each word. "How can they believe in the one," asks Saint Paul, "of whom they have not heard?" (Rom 10:14).

Faith doesn't need to know everything, but it must know something. The Apostles' Creed presents us with a whole list of "somethings," strung together like pearls on a necklace: "conceived by the Holy Spirit, born of the Virgin Mary, suffered under Pontius Pilate … the communion of saints, the forgiveness of sins, the resurrection of the body." We assume that people know all these things and understand them. But in years of teaching the creed, I've discovered a shocking amount of ignorance about the most basic things, even among old-timers in the church.

The church, of course, does not have a corner on ignorance! In 1983 David Helgren, an assistant professor at the University of Miami, gave his

Creed Sermon One – "What Does it Mean to Believe?"

students a geography pop quiz consisting of a blank map of the world with instructions to identify several dozen prominent cities and countries. He expected they wouldn't do well. In fact, they failed epically. Only one in ten could identify Miami on the map; ten students who were actually *from* Miami couldn't find Miami on the map. Half the students couldn't find Chicago and most missed London.[3] We cannot assume that people know the basics, can we?

The creed summarizes the basics of the faith we all need to know. But believing is more than knowing. Many people know the facts of the creed, but will not accept them as true. That is the second aspect of faith—the *acceptance* of something as true. For example, we have all heard of a place called London, England. How many of you have been to London? Most have not. Of those who haven't, how many accept as true that there *is* a London, England? And Big Ben? And Buckingham Palace? And the Tower Bridge?

We normally believe things because of the evidence. We have stories and pictures in books, or the testimony of people who've been there. But "evidence" can be a tricky business. People produce so-called "evidence" for things that may not be true, such as photographs of the Loch Ness Monster or footprints of Sasquatch. On the other hand, many true things don't leave much evidence. So we finally come to a place where evidence runs out and we must decide: will I believe it or not?

It is that way with the creed. There are things in the creed for which there is substantial historical evidence—that there lived a man named Jesus of Nazareth, that he died on a Roman cross, and that his grave was empty. All this is so well attested historically that even enemies of the Christian faith rarely argue about it.

But there are things like the forgiveness of sins, the resurrection of the body, and the life everlasting for which there is no historical evidence—things which can only be addressed by faith. We finally walk by faith and not by sight, said St. Paul (2 Cor 5:7).

The Apostles' Creed brings us to a steep wall. Here we must halt and decide. Here we must show our colors. Will we accept this as true or not?

But even such acceptance is not yet fully saving faith. The Devil himself knows all these things. He could even say "This is most certainly true," but that doesn't make the Devil a Christian! "You believe that there is one God," writes James. "Even the demons believe that—and shudder" (Jas 2:19).

---

3. Gaiser, *Why Geography Matters*, par. 1.

That is the sort of "faith" held by many who like to call themselves Christians. They will not come to worship, nor receive the sacrament. They carry grudges, chase after money, and live what their flesh dictates. They refuse to obey Jesus Christ, or lift a finger to share him with others. Yet if they are challenged, they like to say, "Oh, I still have my faith." Yes, they do. And it is a dead faith, a devil's faith. They have the name of Jesus in their heads, but they will not truly trust him, nor live in service to him in their lives.

That brings us to the third aspect of what it means to believe. Faith is a personal trust in God, a trust which is willing to stake one's life on the promises of Christ. Here we move beyond accepting facts *about* Jesus Christ to having a personal trust *in* Christ. We trust that what he did was for us.

On a human level, it is like the difference between knowing that a certain woman grew up in Indiana, stands five feet, four inches tall, and sings like a bird—and marrying her! I was not content to know some facts about her. One fine day in June of 1968 I went further and put my life in her hands "for better or worse, for richer or poorer, in sickness and in health … till death do us part."

Saving faith means entrusting my life and future to God, becoming a disciple of Jesus Christ, and living out that trust. You demonstrate trust, don't you, whenever you board an airplane? The pilot is a man or woman you have never met, about whom you know little or nothing. Without so much as meeting (or even seeing) that person you board the plane and let him take off down the runway.

We know a great deal more about our Heavenly Father, who made us, and about Jesus Christ, who suffered and died and rose again for us. We have not seen him, but we have heard the news about him. Again and again we have experienced his pardon, his healing, his comfort. We know him to be trustworthy, and we know ourselves richly blessed. His words have come true for us: "Blessed are those who have not seen and yet have believed" (John 20:29).

No, it will not always be easy to go on believing. There are moments when we encounter turbulence—the lights seem to go out and we are left alone and frightened. There are moments when our feelings are flat, when temptations come, and when our moods rebel. In such moments, we need something (someone) on whom our life can be solidly anchored, lest we be blown away like so many tumbleweeds.

Creed Sermon One – "What Does it Mean to Believe?"

How shall we find our bearings and so find life? I heard a story about an arctic explorer who nearly lost his life one night in a snowstorm. He had wandered only a few yards from his hut to retrieve a piece of equipment, but the snow was so thick and the wind so powerful that he not only lost sight of his hut, but lost his sense of direction too. What would he do? If he wandered off in the wrong direction, he could be lost and surely freeze to death before anyone could find him. After thinking for a few moments, he hammered a stake into the ice and attached a length of the rope he was carrying on his belt. Then he began circling, adding more rope as he needed, walking in ever-widening circles until he finally stumbled into the doorway of his hut. He kept his bearings and saved his life!

During the coming weeks, we shall try to "get our bearings" with a long and careful look at the Apostles' Creed, not merely to know it, but also to accept it, and not merely to accept, but finally to trust in the God who made us, loved us, and sent his Son to find us.

Thus staked firmly to him, we shall not fear when the storms of life blind our eyes. We shall walk forward boldly and finally reach the door of our Father's house.

Creed Sermon Two – "I Believe in God the Father"

It happened more than thirty years ago in Ohio, but the memory is still vivid. Our family was in the car, driving home from church after a busy Sunday morning. My mind was shifting into relax mode when suddenly there came a question from my daughter: "Dad, who made God?"

How would you answer my child's question? And who answers yours when you find yourself perplexed by some mystery, or struggling to stay afloat when life's floodwaters swirl around you?

Last Sunday, as we began this sermon series on the Apostles' Creed, we considered what it means to believe. Today we start at ground level and examine how faith answers what my daughter wanted to know: "Who is God?" and "What is he like?"

The first article of the creed gives this answer: "I believe in God the Father Almighty, maker of heaven and earth."

Let's look at the last phrase first: "maker of heaven and earth." These words restate the truth in the very first verse of the Bible: "In the beginning, God created the heavens and the earth" (Gen 1:1). At the time they were written, these words were surprising, even shocking. Most ancient peoples did not understand there to be one creator God. Rather, they envisioned many gods on the vast stage of the world, spirits who took up residence in mountains, lakes and rivers.

When the Israelites arrived in Canaan, they met a people who looked to the surrounding hills to find their gods. The psalmist is attacking that idea when he writes, "I lift up my eyes to the hills—where does my help come from?" Not from the hills! "My help comes from the LORD, the Maker of heaven and earth" (Ps 121:1–2).

We Christians believe what the Psalmist believed. When we say God is "maker," we mean that he is not simply one piece of the creation, but the creator who brought it all into existence.

Creed Sermon Two – "I Believe in God the Father"

A generation ago, Russian cosmonaut Gherman Titov, who shared the atheism of his communist government, returned to earth after an orbital flight and reported, "I did not see anyone there. I did not detect either angels or gods."[1] Well of course not! You won't find God *inside* the Creation as a resident, but *outside* it, just as an author is to be found, not inside the books he writes, but outside.

There in the family car on the way home from church that day, I replied to my daughter, "Honey, He wasn't made at all. Because if someone else had made God (let's call him Mr. X), the next question you'd have to ask is, 'Who made Mr. X?'"

It's an extraordinary idea for a nine-year-old (or any of us) to ponder—that God had no beginning. That idea has great personal consequences for the one who embraces it. A person who confesses God as maker of everything sees the world a whole different way—not as an accidental product of blind chance, but as a masterpiece bearing the signature of God, the Artist and Author.

Those who do not believe in a creator have a hard time explaining how this world came to be. Scientist Robert Jastrow wrote that the universe had a sharply-defined beginning. "For the scientist who has lived by his faith in the power of reason, the story ends like a bad dream. He has scaled the mountain of ignorance; he is about to conquer the highest peak; as he pulls himself over the final rock, he is greeted by a band of theologians who have been sitting there for centuries."[2]

You'd think what the Apostles' Creed affirms here at the start would be obvious and impressive—the world was created. But many people these days seem unimpressed by the created world. We have surrounded ourselves with man's inventions—rockets that reach the outer edge of the solar system, robots that can clean your swimming pool, computers that can defeat grandmasters in chess, and tiny cameras that explore the insides of our blood vessels.

If all this man-made machinery has sucked the wonder out of the creation for us, shouldn't we take time to stop, to smell the roses and gaze at the moon? If we marvel at the things the human mind can make, shouldn't we ask, in my daughter's fashion, "But who made our minds?"

Yet even this would not be enough to know God. We may spend a lifetime pondering the universe, and it might convince us that there is both

---

1. Biedryczky, *"Comrade Gagarin,"* par. 7.
2. Jastrow, *God and the Astronomers*, 116.

intelligence and purpose at work, but the identity of that intelligence would remain a mystery.

It's like the story of Goldilocks and the Three Bears. Imagine that you are Goldilocks. You find yourself in the woods. You come to a clearing and discover a large log cabin sitting vacant. There are flowers in the planter and a wisp of smoke curling from the chimney. "Someone made this," you know without being told. That Someone is intelligent and strong. And that Someone is living here, you can plainly see. You don't yet know who it is, or what the owner will think of you if you go inside.

Our world, like that cabin, has been built by Someone intelligent and strong. Most people can see that, but they are in the dark about who it is. Who is the Someone that made heaven and earth, and what does this Someone think of me?

The Creed goes a step further, and gives this Maker a name full of meaning. "I believe in God the Father." Jesus himself taught us that. "When you pray, say, 'Our Father.'" What difference does it make to call him Father?

The chief freight in the word Father is the relationship it describes. It says that God is not some Star Wars "Force," but an intelligent being who can communicate with us. Further, this intelligent being is no stranger, but the very one who gave us life, knows us intimately, and loves and cares for each of us personally.

We parents know how such love feels, don't we? For we remember the day that our child entered this world. When my firstborn was wrapped in a blanket and laid on the scale in the delivery room, I remember bending over her to marvel at her tiny fingers and her soft hair. It was in that moment, more than any other since, that I finally got a glimpse of the exquisite love God has for each of us.

It works the other way around too. Children, if your earthly father is a good, caring daddy, can you begin to see, in him, a glimpse of what God must be like as he provides, protects, and corrects us?

"Father"—what an amazing thing to say of God! When we say it, we confess that the same God who is greater than the galaxies is small enough to enter my sickroom as I gasp for breath, intimate enough to care about the trifling things that make up the greatest part of my life—the headaches and toothaches, the mealtimes and playtimes, the furnace that needs fixing, the back-to-school shopping trip, and my every shifting mood.

In other words, although there are billions of us, God knows each individual. That's why, in his Small Catechism, Luther personalizes things: "I

Creed Sermon Two – "I Believe in God the Father"

believe that God has made me . . . that He has given me my body . . . and all my senses, and still takes care of them."[3] When we call God "Father," we confess not only that he created the stars and planets in the vastness of space, but that he created and still cares about me, even me!

It is not easy to keep on believing this. The great French painter, Paul Cezanne, during his difficult and often lonely life, used to utter a stereotyped groan, "Life is terrible."[4] Have we not all felt that sometimes? Loved ones die. Dreams are dashed. News stories shock us. With dreadful regularity we hear about mass shootings at schools and churches, shopping centers and theaters. We see people who are scoundrels and cold-hearted calculators basking in abundance, while some simple, decent folks are doing without.

When it happens to others, we must not make light of the neighbor's pain and say, "Well, God is a good and loving Father; change your attitude," for the day will surely come when we have our own trouble and we understand their tears at last. Even today, some in our own congregation are facing trials both frightening and frustrating.

God is our Father, but he does not remove every evil with the snap of his finger, nor does he make the answer to every prayer simple and satisfying to our minds. We will hurt. And we will not always understand. How then can we go on calling God Father when life feels terrible?

In the end, I believe doing that is possible only for those who know him through the Son, Jesus Christ. It is Jesus, finally, who shows us the heart of the Father working even in the pain and death that meet us. Jesus himself rarely used the word "God," but much more often addressed God as "Father" in his prayers, especially as he suffered!

There in the Garden of Gethsemane it was "My Father, if it is possible, may this cup be taken from me. Yet not as I will, but as you will" (Matt 26:39). The next day on the cross, at the end of a painful, bloody ordeal, as Jesus came to the moment of his death, he said it again, "Father, into your hands I commit my spirit" (Luke 23:46). Though all around Him grew dark, still he knew that Father's heart was beating for him.

The resurrection on Easter morning was the Father's answer to that Son. It is the answer he gives to all who come to him as children and entrust themselves to his care. One old woman who had been through many trials said, "I don't know why, but I do know who!" She knew God as Father. Do you?

---

3. Luther, *Small Catechism*, 15.
4. Thielicke, *I Believe*, 16.

Come to him this morning. Come as a child, simply and trustingly. He will not turn you away. If God still feels frightening and distant to you, do not come alone. Come hand in hand with Jesus. Conrad Meyer wrote, "For two of us, instead of one, abide—I and the thorn-crowned brother by my side."[5]

Place your hand in his, and with his help you will be able to say, and truly mean, these words: "I believe in God the Father."

---

5. Thielicke, *I Believe*, 25.

Creed Sermon Three – "I Believe in Jesus Christ"

IMAGINE A WARM AFTERNOON under a cloudless sky. Jesus and His small band of followers leave a trail of dust behind them as they trudge down a dirt path toward Caesarea Philippi. They draw to a halt for a rest. Jesus turns to eye them. "Who do people say the Son of Man is?" he asks (Matt 16:13).

Their answers tumble over one another in a torrent of eager words. "Oh, different things, rabbi!" "One fellow said John the Baptist." "I heard someone say Elijah." "Other people have guessed Jeremiah." An upraised hand from Jesus silences them. "But what about you?" he asks. "Who do you say I am?" (Matt 6:15).

It was the greatest of questions for them. Their lives were, quite literally, hanging on the answer. It is still the great question today. Your identity and your eternal destiny hang on the answer you give. "Who do you say that Jesus is?"

In America, people of different Christian denominations and even non-Christians have adopted and used him for a variety of purposes. The figure of Jesus has, in ways, become disconnected from traditional Christian doctrine and acquired a life of its own.

Jesus has been appropriated to champion women's rights. He has been espoused as a favorite political philosopher. Americans regularly enlist Jesus, their ultimate arbiter of value, as the standard-bearer for their views and causes. What would Jesus drive? What would Jesus eat? Whom would Jesus bomb?

Today we begin exploring the second article of the creed, the one dealing with Jesus Christ and His work. "This article," declared Luther in his Large Catechism, "is a very rich and far-reaching one ... The entire Gospel we preach depends on our thorough grasp of this article."[1]

1. Luther, *Large Catechism*, 72.

Most Certainly True

We begin simply with the question Jesus asked his disciples: "Who do people say I am?" The answer to that question is the dividing line that separates the Christian from the rest of the world. For a "Christian" by his very name is not simply a nice person who tries to live by the rules nor merely a theist who acknowledges that there's a god in charge somewhere—a "man upstairs" who runs the world. A Christian is a confessor of and a believer in Jesus as the Messiah, the Christ. A Christian is a "Christ-connected" person who holds Jesus of Nazareth to be the Savior and Lord of his life.

It's not an exaggeration to say that people all over the world have heard of him by now, and that everyone who has heard of him has an opinion about who he is. Even his enemies are impressed by him. Atheist writer Albert Camus said that Jesus was so humane, "I think pretty well of Him." Soviet poet Yevgeny Yevtushenko confessed, "Not that I am a follower of Christ, but I like His manner!"[2]

Some in other religions have a respect for him and an appreciation of His impact that shames us who have grown so accustomed to his story. In the movie *Gandhi,* the story of the well-known Hindu resistance leader in India, Gandhi and a young Christian clergyman happen upon a group of ruffians who threaten them. The clergyman wants to turn around, but Gandhi gently rebukes him with the reminder that Jesus said to turn the other cheek and not resist evil. Gandhi had read the words of Jesus and brought them to mind more readily than that clergyman.

Everyone, it seems, is impressed with Jesus! The Jews acknowledge him as a great Rabbi. Muslims call him one of the prophets. I met a Sikh man in a turban at the airport in Oakland. He told me that Sikhs incorporate some of Jesus' teachings too.

That is where many people stop. Yes, they say, Jesus was a great teacher. So were Buddha and Mohammad and Confucius. "All those teachers were for loving your neighbor, and so am I," they say. "What does it matter who said it so long as we do it?" I remember a man who said that to me and then concluded, "My religion is the Ten Commandments and the Golden Rule!"

But isn't that just where we have a problem? We have never consistently followed the advice of all those great moral teachers. Which of us keeps the commandments fully? Who always lives by the Golden Rule? We need more than a *teacher* to instruct us. We need a *savior* who can rescue and change us! The question Jesus asked the disciples was not, "What do men say that I *teach*?" but rather "Who do men say that I *am*?"

2. Thielicke, *I Believe,* 74.

Creed Sermon Three – "I Believe in Jesus Christ"

Open your hymnals to the back cover and look at the creed's second paragraph—the article about Jesus Christ. It contains nothing of what Jesus taught. Instead, it's about who Jesus is and what he has done.

Today we zero in on the first phrase, just nine words long: "and in Jesus Christ, His only Son, our Lord." Each name, each title, draws the curtain back further to reveal him to us.

First is the name Jesus. "You are to give him the name Jesus," the angel said to Joseph, "because he will save his people from their sins" (Matt 1:21). The Savior he is, not just another teacher. The Buddha directed people to an eight-fold path to find life, but Jesus said that he himself is that path—"I am the way and the truth and the life" (John 14:6).

Second, we call him "Christ." That's not a name, but a title—the Messiah, "the Anointed One." The word "Christ" says he is the King the Jews had waited for all those long centuries. Peter realized it that day on the road to Caesarea Philippi. Scarcely had Jesus finished asking "Who do you say I am?" when Peter responded, "You are the Christ" (Matt 16:16). It was an astonishing confession. Peter was saying, "Our waiting is over. God's kingdom has come. You are the Messiah!"

Third, Christians say He is God's "only Son." Which of us ever gives this title much thought? But stop and think about the meaning. One day there turns up among the Jews a man who goes about forgiving sins and saying, "Before Abraham was born, I am," (John 8:58) and "You will see the Son of Man . . . coming on the clouds" (Matt 27:64). What sort of man would say such things? Mohammad never did. Krishna never did. Confucius never did.

But Jesus did. And in so doing he laid claim to being God among us—the Son of God come down to earth. "What this man said," writes C. S. Lewis, "was, quite simply, the most shocking thing that has ever been uttered by human lips . . . either this man was, and is, the Son of God, or else a madman."[3] We Christians believe that he is what he said—the Son of God.

Finally, we call him "Lord." A lord is someone who is in charge, the master of another's life. The Christians who first confessed "Jesus is Lord" lived in a world where the Roman Emperor was the supreme ruler. People everywhere were commanded, on pain of death, to say "Caesar is lord!" For many, owning Jesus as the true "Lord" was a confession that cost them their lives.

---

3. Lewis, *Mere Christianity*, 55–6.

But I have left the most crucial thing out. Do you see it? One crucial three-letter word on which everything else hinges. The little word is *our*— "His only Son, our Lord."

Once again, Luther personalizes it in the Small Catechism: "I believe that Jesus Christ . . . is my Lord."[4] Mine. Yours. Ours!

There's a world of difference, isn't there, between saying Jesus is merely *a* lord and confessing him as *our* Lord? It's possible to say the words of this creed, to parrot them from memory, and yet to keep our distance from it.

Perhaps a picture will help. Many of us have walked through a nursing home. The people that line the hallways in their wheelchairs are certainly real people, each with a name and a history. To the average visitor, they are just "old people"— strangers. You walk past them with a smile, and keep a distance. But today, your visit to that nursing home is different. You are there to see your own family member who just moved in. That old man in the wheelchair is your father who read stories to you as you sat on his knee. That old woman waving at you down the hall is your grandmother, who used to comb your hair and make you cookies! Everything has changed. That nursing home is a different place, because this person is yours.

Is it not so with Christ? Those who wander into a church and hear the reciting of an ancient creed may find it all strange. They smile and keep a distance. Even for us who have been in the church for many years, the worship may be a dry routine and the creed a stale formula, until the moment we realize that this Lord we confess is ours, that he loved us, died and rose for us, and will one day come back for us.

The Jesus in this creed is alive, and he is ours. He would come to each of us sitting here now and take up residence within. Luigi Pirandello, the Italian dramatist, wrote a play called *Six Characters in Search of an Author*. In that play, a group of actors have assembled on a stage and are rehearsing their lines. They are interrupted by the arrival of six strangers who say they have been side-tracked. When the stage manager asks what they want. They clamor that their great desire is to live inside the actors themselves!

This very morning, Jesus stands at the door of your life and knocks persistently. He would come in and live inside you, inside me. Will we acknowledge him, and answer the question he now directs at us: "Who do you say I am?"

Others have known the answer. "You are the Christ," said Peter on the dusty path. "Look, the Lamb of God, who takes away the sin of the world!"

---

4. Luther, *Small Catechism*, 16.

Creed Sermon Three – "I Believe in Jesus Christ"

said John the Baptist by the Jordan (John 1:29). "He is Christ the Lord," announced the angel over Bethlehem (Luke 2:11). "Surely this man was the Son of God!" confessed the centurion at the cross (Mark 15:39).

What will you say?

Hear the Good News with your ears. Believe it in your hearts. Confess it with your lips. If you share this faith, will you say so now? Confess the words after me: "I believe in Jesus Christ, His only Son, our Lord."

And will you now pray after me? "Lord Jesus, come and live in me. Shine through me, now and always. Amen."

Creed Sermon Four – "I Believe in the Virgin Birth"

We are examining the Apostles' Creed, phrase by phrase.

If a poll were taken to discover what part of the story of Jesus is best known, it would likely be the Christmas story. Usually we think about this story in December. But here in the middle of the year, let's take a look with the Christmas wrappings removed.

In the creed, the Christmas story is summed up in a pair of matched phrases, each five words long. Jesus was, the creed says, "Conceived by the Holy Spirit, born of the Virgin Mary." It's important to separate these twin affirmations from the sentiment that so often surrounds them. Of course we like babies. Our hearts are drawn to the story of his birth. But what do we really mean when we confess these strange words?

Some critics call the Virgin Birth a "fairy tale." Defenders of the faith disagree. Accordingly, in some places this issue has become a test of orthodoxy. A man who was considered for the call to a church in Ohio was finally rejected for this very issue. He would not affirm his belief in the Virgin Birth.

I believe in the Virgin Birth—the "First Miracle" of the Christian faith, on which the others hinge. But I also believe that confessing it means more than saying "God can do miracles" and leaving it at that. These phrases touch the Gospel itself—our understanding of who Jesus is and what he has done.

Let's take each phrase in turn. First: "Conceived by the Holy Spirit." What this says, literally, is that Jesus did not have a human father. Mary became pregnant, not through Joseph, but through the agency of the Holy Spirit.

Some people who object like to say that the early Christians believed this because they were ignorant of the facts of nature and did not realize this was scientifically impossible. But that is simply nonsense. The Bible says

Creed Sermon Four – "I Believe in the Virgin Birth"

that when Joseph heard that Mary was pregnant, he decided to break off the engagement. Why? Because he knew very well how pregnancy happens. So did those Jews who later taunted Jesus about his parentage. When Joseph finally accepted the fact that Mary's pregnancy was due, not to promiscuity, but to the intervention of God, he knew that it could only be a miracle.

But what does that miracle mean?

It means that God himself has come among us in this man Jesus. The Creator of the world entered it as one of its creatures. Think about that. It is, on a grand scale, something like what happened in Chicago years ago. There in 1981, Chicago's new mayor, Jane Byrne, announced that she would find out what life in the ghetto was like. So she moved into the Cabrini-Green projects, much to the astonishment of the people in her city.

Perhaps an even more accurate parallel is the story that unfolds in a 1968 movie entitled *The Antkeeper*. It's about a man who owns an ant farm and is dismayed to see his ants in chaos and conflict. He decides to help by becoming an ant himself and entering his own ant farm! The end result, predictably, is that the others ants turn on him and kill him, though he was trying to help them.

We will return to that part of the story later in this series, but for now we focus on the miracle we call the Incarnation—the Son of God became a man and entered our world.

The people who met Jesus during his earthly life perceived that though he was a man like others in appearance, he was also noticeably different. There was an "otherness" about him, as if he were from outside the world! "What kind of man is this?" asked his own disciples (Matt 8:27).

Perhaps you have noticed in the Gospel record that when people came close to touch Him, it was not his hand they seized, but his cloak. Familiarity gave way to wonder, and finally to awe, as Thomas knelt down and confessed, "My Lord and my God" (John 20:28).

This Jesus was clearly different from other people in his sinlessness. He was accused of being crazy and of being in league with the Devil. But no one ever accused him of a sin and made it stick. That very thing the angel had predicted to Mary: "The Holy Spirit will come upon you and the power of the Most High will overshadow you. So the holy one to be born will be called the Son of God" (Luke 1:35). Accordingly we confess, "I believe … He was conceived by the Holy Spirit."

But immediately the creed adds a second phrase, the companion of the first: "Born of the Virgin Mary." What this phrase says, literally, is that though he had God as his Father, he had a human mother. He was born in the normal way all of us are.

That mention of Mary, by the way, is not so much a statement about *her* as it is about *him*. He did not arrive, like Superman, in a space capsule from the planet Krypton. No. He was *born*. At a particular spot on earth, in a particular moment in history. To a mother who went through labor and delivery.

Some in the early church could not believe that Jesus was really a human being. There grew up a heresy called Docetism, which taught that Jesus was only masquerading as a man, but was in fact a kind of phantom. The Docetists taught, accordingly, that Jesus could not really experience what we humans experience, nor die as we die.

The Apostles' Creed is the church's answer to them—an affirmation that Jesus was as fully human as we are. He got thirsty, hungry, and fearful. He laughed, He cried, and he was tempted to sin. He could suffer and die, and finally he did.

No other religion besides Christianity says such astounding things about human flesh. Hindus and Buddhists regard the flesh as an evil, an encumbrance to be shaken off. We Christians say that God not only created flesh. He entered into it!

The church has always held these two phrases together. Like the harmony of the treble clef and the bass clef is the harmony of our confession: "Conceived by the Holy Spirit, born of the Virgin Mary." So we sing that he is our "Beautiful Savior, King of Creation, Son of God and Son of Man."

Still, someone might ask, so what? My life and yours must still go on. We must endure our pains and uncertainties. What does all this theology have to do with me right now?

First of all, we Christians believe that all this happened for us. Jesus Christ was conceived by the Holy Spirit and born of the Virgin Mary in order to rescue us.

We confess that in Jesus, God himself plunged into this world like a diver who strips off his clothing and plunges into the water with a splash. Down he rushes from the light and the warmth at the surface to the cold darkness beneath, down through increasing pressure into a deadly region of ooze and slime, then up again, back to color and light, his lungs bursting, until suddenly he breaks the surface again, holding in his hand the dripping, precious thing he went down to retrieve.

Creed Sermon Four – "I Believe in the Virgin Birth"

If the words of the creed are true, then this was the central event in the world's long history, and the fate of every human life hinges on whether or not we allow him to grab hold of us and bring us back up to "color and light" again.

This sermon is no mere string of statements but the proclamation that God has gone to the greatest of lengths to rescue us and the appeal to build our lives upon it. We may see ourselves as unspeakably precious to him!

Second, this creed is to give birth to a particular deed—that we regard every other life as infinitely precious, just as God regarded us. The mission of a "rescued people" is that they, in turn, become rescuers of others, for if God did not despise our human flesh, but entered it, so we must not despise the neighbor, however lowly, but respect him and seek to enter his world with the love of God.

When we Christians gather for worship, it is to be equipped and then launched into the neighborhood, the city, and the larger world. It is why Christians have started hospitals and orphanages, alcohol treatment facilities, pregnancy care centers, and homes for the developmentally disabled. For the same reason our chaplains enter battlefields, emergency rooms at the hospital, and prison cells. It also moves Christian teens to take blankets to homeless people under bridges, women to make pillow case dresses for the poor in Africa, and servant teams to travel to Appalachia.

All of this happens because of Christmas, all because the Son of God emptied himself, taking the form of a servant, and being born in the likeness of men.

If we mattered that much to him, then others matter that much to us, and when we serve the neighbor, it is, in fact, still the hands of Jesus that touch them through us.

It is not only in December that we pray it, but at all times and in all places: "O holy child of Bethlehem, descend to us we pray. Cast out our sin and enter in, be born in us today."

Creed Sermon Five –
"I Believe He Suffered and Died"

WHEN WE READ THE biography of some famous person, the author usually supplies a mountain of details about that life—the ancestors, the parents, the siblings, the schooling and work, the accomplishments and failures and feelings. Carl Sandburg's biography of Abraham Lincoln, for example, is six volumes long.

By comparison, the life of Jesus in the Gospels is presented in extreme brevity. The longest of them takes up only forty pages or so in my Bible. The Gospels offer only the barest framework of a life that truly could fill a whole world of books.

When we come to the Apostles' Creed, we find the briefest statement of all. His life from birth to death is summarized in only fifteen words: "born of the Virgin Mary, suffered under Pontius Pilate, was crucified, died, and was buried."

The writers of the creed did not suffer from literary anemia, nor were they embarrassed about their subject. Instead, they were focusing on the purpose of the life of Jesus Christ. This was a man born to die.

His suffering and death were not the unfortunate end of a promising career. The suffering and death *were* his career – the purpose for which he came. "The good shepherd lays down his life for the sheep" (John 10:11) is how Jesus put it.

His suffering and dying are the key signature of the church and every Christian. Our chief symbol is the cross, the instrument of his execution. Our most important week, "Holy Week," re-traces his steps through the final week of his life, which ends in his crucifixion.

During these weeks, we are trying to get beneath the surface of the Apostles' Creed. What does it mean when we confess that he "suffered

Creed Sermon Five – "I Believe He Suffered and Died"

under Pontius Pilate, was crucified, died, and was buried?" If we can understand his suffering, we can begin to understand our own. The question Jesus asked in agony on the cross is the one every one of us asks if we suffer long enough and deeply enough: "My God, why?"

Why did Jesus suffer? First, and most simply, he suffered because he is really human. All real humans suffer. There are physical ailments—sickness, hunger and thirst, and a wide array of aches and pains. There are emotional traumas—crushing fears and haunting loneliness, dreadful bereavement, and more. There are spiritual sufferings galore at the hands of our doubts and temptations, and the desperate search for God. He suffers them all because he is human like the rest of us.

His suffering and death did not take place in someone's imagination. Nor in some faraway corner. They happened publicly, at the center of history. "Suffered under Pontius Pilate" locates it in time. Pilate was a real, historical character known not only to the biblical writers but to secular historians. Pilate was the Roman governor of Judea from the years AD 26–36. The death of Jesus took place in Pilate's third year—in April of AD 29. Pilate enters the picture because at that time the Jews were under Roman rule and were not allowed to execute anyone.

Only the Romans could do that.

When his suffering was over, they said of Jesus what will finally be said of us all: "dead and buried." Do you take his death for granted? Not everyone today does. A billion Muslims say Jesus did not die, but was taken directly to heaven.

Not everyone in the earliest days did either. The rumor circulated that Jesus had only fainted from loss of blood on the cross. They said that the Romans, mistakenly believing him dead, allowed his family to take his body down and bury him. So goes the "Swoon Theory."

But it couldn't have been. The Romans were good at killing people. Executions were their specialty. Witnesses that day saw them make sure of Jesus with the violent thrust of a spear. "He's dead all right!" Jesus suffered and died because he was a real human being. That's the first reason.

There was a second, deeper, reason. Jesus suffered because he loved. If someone loves another person, he wants to share what that person's experiences. "Where you go, I will go . . . Where you die, I will die" said Ruth to Naomi (Ruth 1:17).

We are tempted, so he submits to temptation. We grow exhausted from the schedule and lack of sleep. He does too. We wrestle with God and cry out in despair. He takes up our cry with his own lips on the cross. "My God, why have you forsaken me?" (Matt 27:46). We die, and he determines that he will die with us. "I lay down my life ... No one takes it from me, but I lay it down of my own accord" (John 10:18).

Love suffers with the beloved. During the Second World War, the German army was besieged at Stalingrad. The army was doomed, and a last planeload of evacuees was to fly out before the net finally closed. The chaplain was offered a place on the plane. He had a large family, and he was suffering from painful frostbite. But the chaplain refused. He had come this far with the men, he said. He could not leave them in their darkest hour. He loved them, and in that hour they came to know it with certainty.

That is why Jesus lets himself be found on all of life's battlefields among all sufferers. He loves with a love that enters all our sufferings. He did it all, says the catechism, "that I may be His own, and live under Him in His kingdom, and serve Him in everlasting righteousness, innocence, and blessedness."[1]

But there is a third reason for his suffering, which goes beyond what any of us can do. He suffers because of our sins. Isn't that why the creed is very specific about the *way* he dies? He does not die of pneumonia or cancer. He is not killed in an accident. He is crucified.

Historian Paul Maier notes that crucifixions were done in such a way as to humiliate the victims, most of whom were stripped naked, taunted by the crowd, and left to endure cramped muscles and crawling insects before they died, sometimes after several days of torture. Crucifixion was never done to Roman citizens. It was reserved for slaves, pirates, and other notorious criminals.[2]

Jesus died a "criminal's death" because he was truly dying for crimes—not his, but ours. All the crimes we have committed against God and against each other from the moment of Adam and Eve's rebellion until this very moment. The Bible says, "God made him who had no sin to be sin for us, so that in him, we might become the righteousness of God" (2 Cor 5:21). It was a great exchange. He took what is ours and gave us what is his. That's why, when we remember the day of his death, we call it Good Friday. It was bad for him, but very good for us.

People who believe in him discover that his suffering and death changes their own. We still suffer, but the bitterness and sting is gone. We

---

1. Luther, *Small Catechism*, 16.
2. Maier, *First Easter*, 77.

Creed Sermon Five – "I Believe He Suffered and Died"

still die, but death has become a door, and even as we grieve, we do so in hope and confidence. Because he died for us, we determine that we shall live, no longer for ourselves, but for him.

It was a cold, gray Memorial Day in a cemetery in New York. An elderly man had just placed flowers on his wife's grave and stood there in silence. He noticed that standing nearby was a young man in his twenties, silent, lost in thought. On an impulse the older man went over to him and placed an arm on the young man's shoulder. Looking down at the headstone of an older man, he asked in a kindly way, "Was this your father?" "No," said the young man, "not a relative at all. In fact, we did not know each other."

There was a pause. The older man looked bewildered, so the younger man went on. "Twenty-two years ago, there was an apartment fire not far from here. One of the firemen went in, found a child trapped on the second floor, and passed the baby out the window to another fireman. A moment later, the wall collapsed and the fireman was killed. This man was the fireman. I was the baby. I come here each year to remember that because this man died, I am alive."

Isn't that why we are here today? To remember and confess that Jesus suffered and died that we might live. We confess it, not with sadness, but with a joy inexpressible. He who once was dead is now alive forevermore, and so are we!

Even now he is among us, bidding us to bring him our burdens, and give them to him. Let us remember the price he paid, and vow with gratitude that we will make the most of the life he gives us.

Creed Sermon Six – "I Believe He Descended into Hell"

Today we come to the most mysterious, least understood part of the creed: "He descended into hell." What do we mean by these words?

A few years ago I asked a random sample of our members what they understood when they spoke that portion of the creed. I got quite a variety of answers, including the admission by several that they were completely mystified.

One stumbling block is that word "hell." It sounds archaic to modern ears. Try to have a serious discussion of hell nowadays, and someone may ask whether we accept that medieval picture of bubbling cauldrons and demons with pitchforks. Someone else might chime in, "I think we have our hell right here on earth!"

Even convinced Christians have their misgivings. It sounds strange when Jesus, the friend of sinners, speaks so strongly about "eternal fire" and "outer darkness," about "weeping and gnashing of teeth."

Jesus we understand. But who feels certain what hell is all about? Can it really be a binding article of faith when the official creed of the church puts them both together into the same phrase, "He descended into hell"?

I will not say that this phrase is the most important one in the creed. It is not. No other part of the creed has such meager support in the Bible. No other part has been subjected to such disagreement as this one. Nevertheless, if we take the creed seriously, we will not bypass these words nor brush them lightly aside just because they sound strange to our modern ears. For like the rest of the creed, these words too were meant to express a part of the good news of Jesus.

Creed Sermon Six – "I Believe He Descended into Hell"

Over the centuries there have been at least four different understandings of this part of the creed. Each is worth examining, for each one speaks some truth about Jesus.

The first view is that the words "He descended into hell" are just another way of saying "He went into death." The first person I phoned in my survey said that: "He went to the grave. He died."

In the Old Testament, the destiny of all the dead was summed up in a single Hebrew word: *sheol*. That's a vague term that means something like "the hereafter" with the understanding that its direction was down, not up. Good and bad, righteous and unrighteous alike, went "down to *sheol*." There they remained in a weak, shadowy existence. The Greek word transliterated "Hades" used here and there in the New Testament means something similar. That's how some people understand these words in the creed. One hymnal has an asterisk by the phrase that refers worshipers to the bottom of the page where they can say, "He descended to the dead."

Indeed, Jesus really died. But the creed itself has already said so with the words "was crucified, died, and was buried." This phrase must mean something more.

The second view is that the words mean he suffered the pains of hell itself on that Good Friday. That is, he went to hell and suffered there so we would not have to. The core idea behind the word hell in the New Testament is separation from God, the exclusion from his presence Paul described in 2 Thessalonians. All the images of darkness, of fire, and of weeping and gnashing of teeth are pictures of what it is like to be cut off from God.

Those who say we "suffer hell right here on earth" are partly right. Not only after death, but even in the middle of life we can feel such a separation. I asked one woman whose husband had left her how she was doing. "I'm in hell," she said. "Right now, life is hell and I don't know when it will get better."

Did not Jesus himself have such a moment on the cross when he cried out, "My God, why have you forsaken me?" He who suffered for our sins also suffered the hellish separation from God that sin produces. That's what another one of my interviewees told me: "The descent into hell means he experienced the worst that people can suffer."

But it was not understood that way among the earliest Christians. Most of them heard, in this phrase, not a reference to his suffering, but a declaration of his victory, a victory that brought rescue. So I must share a third understanding, a very common one in the early church: Christ descended into hell to bring salvation to Old Testament believers.

Not a single one of the folks I interviewed saw it this way. But many early Christians did. During the first centuries after Christ, many were asking, "What about those who died before Jesus came? What happened to Jacob and Moses? To Abraham, Isaiah, and the rest of them? They had waited for Christ's coming, but never saw it. Are they now abandoned in the world of the dead? If not, how will they get to heaven unless Christ goes to rescue them?

So it happened that many early Christians understood the descent into hell as a sort of rescue mission, like the one attempted by the U.S. government in 1981 to free the hostages held at the embassy in Tehran, Iran. Fifty-two diplomats were held for more than a year. The mission failed when one of the rescue helicopters crashed in the desert.

That mission failed, but this rescue mission by Christ was successful, as early believers pictured it. Artists who drew picture on the walls of the catacombs in Rome pictured a victorious Christ carrying a banner, standing at the edge of a trench, and pulling up by the hand a procession of pre-Christian saints. It was called the "harrowing of hell," and it is still the official teaching of the Greek Orthodox Church.

In a way, all Christians share that understanding of the Gospel. It is good, not only for us who are privileged to live after Christ, but also for those who lived before, who only saw it from afar. "Abraham rejoiced at the thought of seeing my day," said Jesus. "He saw it and was glad" (John 8:56).

But did our Lord personally conduct such a rescue mission after his death on the cross? We must finally ask: "What does the Bible say?"

It won't be hard to check on this. There is only one passage that is appealed to for this phrase in the creed. It is a notoriously difficult passage, 1 Peter 3:18–20. There we read, "For Christ died for sins, once for all, the righteous for the unrighteous, to bring you to God. He was put to death in the body but made alive by the Spirit, through whom also he went and preached to the spirits in prison who disobeyed long ago when God waited patiently in the days of Noah while the ark was being built."

The Bible says here that Christ, sometime after his death, "went and preached to the spirits in prison." Who are these "spirits"? Probably not dead humans. The word "spirits" used this way almost always refers to angelic beings, most likely the ones we would call demons. For they are in a "prison" of some sort. The letter of Jude tells us that the angels who rebelled

Creed Sermon Six – "I Believe He Descended into Hell"

against God are confined in "chains" until the last judgment (Jude 6). So this is not *sheol*, the general realm of the dead, but specifically hell—the place Jesus said was prepared for the Devil and his angels.

Jesus went, says this text, and "preached." The Greek word is not the usual word for "preach the Gospel," but another word that means "make an announcement or a proclamation." Jesus would certainly not be preaching the Gospel to the demons! Rather he is making an announcement to them. What can Jesus be announcing to the demons, unless it is his victory over them?

So it is that there is a fourth view of the descent into hell. It says that after his death, Jesus went there and announced his victory over hell and Satan. Martin Luther took this view, as do many others. He preached about it on Easter Day of 1533 in the city of Torgau. There he explained that after burial, Christ descended into hell, destroyed the Devil's power, and captured the colors like a conquering hero!

Our church has taken this view of it, though we do not deny the truths contained in the others. As we confess it, the death of Christ ended his sufferings for us. When on the cross Jesus said, "It is finished" (John 19:30), he declared that the task of paying for our sins was accomplished, finalized. The descent into hell and all that followed are the beginning of his triumph and glory, and the end of power for all our worst enemies.

This message is more a lecture than a sermon, for this is a difficult subject that requires exploring and explaining.

Yet I believe there *is* a sermon here too, a message of encouragement and hope for the daily battles we must fight. Satan and hell continue to be real enemies to us, even though they have been defeated. One southern preacher likened a defeated Satan to an alligator that has been caught, tied up, and hauled into the boat. "You still got to be careful," said that preacher, "because when that 'gator thrashes, his tail can break your leg!"

Yes, the devil still thrashes at us. Yes, life is hellish when our sins separate us from the Father. Yes, death still terrifies us in our times of weakness and doubt. At such moments, can we not take comfort in those words "He descended into hell"?

Hell is real, but its power is gone. Jesus holds the keys that unlock it. On Palm Sunday, Jesus entered Jerusalem to destroy Satan's power. And he did. No need to fear him anymore. The Devil is a caged beast who can only roar at us from behind his bars. Neither hell nor the Devil can harm those who cling to Christ in faith. So cling to him, and rejoice!

Creed Sermon Seven –
"I Believe He Rose from the Dead"

THERE IS NO OTHER day like Easter. And no better news than *this* news, announced by the angel long ago, confessed by the church all these centuries: "The third day He rose again from the dead."

If you take time to count, you'll find that there are 111 words in the Apostles' Creed, and this phrase brings us to the very center - word fifty-six. That's appropriate, for this article—the resurrection of Jesus—is the very center of our Christian faith.

Everything we believe hangs on it, revolves around it. Paul said it long ago: "If Christ has not been raised, our preaching is useless and so is your faith" (1 Cor 15:14). In the Small Catechism, Luther grounds the truth of everything else on this foundation: "Just as He is risen from the dead, and lives and reigns to all eternity, this is most certainly true."[1]

Think of it this way: a woman sets out to sew her husband's torn shirt by hand. She takes a needle and threads it. But she cannot simply start in stitching. First she must make a knot to hold the thread in place; otherwise, it will eventually pull apart. The resurrection of Jesus is the knot that holds the fabric of our faith firmly in place.

What do we mean when we say "He rose again from the dead"? Let's make clear what we do *not* mean. To say "Jesus rose from the dead" does not mean he lives on only in the hearts of those who loved him as a warm feeling or a happy memory. Nor do we mean that he changed from a fleshly human being into a disembodied spirit, hovering in the cool air of the garden. No, his dead body itself came to life again. When Jesus rose, it was not as a memory or a ghost! It was as his body with fingers and toes and a digestive system that could share a meal of fish with His astonished disciples.

---

1. Luther, *Small Catechism*, 17.

Creed Sermon Seven – "I Believe He Rose from the Dead"

Nevertheless, the Bible everywhere portrays the resurrection of Jesus as a totally new thing, an event unique in history, something that had not happened before. It is true, of course, that the Bible reports about others who came back from the dead—Lazarus, the widow's son, and the daughter of Jairus, for example. Those were miracles, certainly, but in each case what happened was a resuscitation by which the dead person came back exactly as he or she was before. For them, death was merely postponed.

With Jesus, it is different. He rises, never again to die! Yes, his risen body is very like the one he had before. He can still eat. He can still be touched. His flesh even bears the wound marks in his hands, feet, and side. But there is something different, something more about his risen body. He can suddenly appear in a locked room, and just as suddenly vanish. People who have known him for years have trouble recognizing him. Finally, forty days later, his body is lifted up from the earth into a different mode of existence.

All of this is what we mean when we confess the words "The third day He rose again from the dead." But it is not enough to know what these words mean. The more important question is, "What do they mean *to you*?" What difference does believing this make in your life?

Some teens were sitting in a church basement playing a game that required players to draw a card and answer honestly whatever question was printed on it. A freshman girl drew her card and read these words: "Jesus Christ rose from the dead. What does this have to do with your life?" She paused, uncertain, and everyone waited. It was hard or her to answer. Had you drawn that card, what would you say? I ask you in all seriousness, for this is not a game. It is at the heart of what makes each one of us joyful or sorrowful, hopeful or despairing.

May I tell you what I might say? It means to me, first of all, that as we sit here in church, we are not remembering a dead hero. No, for he is alive! He meets us here and now, as surely as he met the astonished disciples in that locked room Easter evening.

It means, further, that our prayers are not arrows shot into the dark, swallowed up into a void. No, there is an ear that hears each one, and there will surely be an answer. Even more wonderfully, it means that the shameful sins we have confessed with tears are not still following us around like some hungry stray cat. They are gone forever, buried with him as surely as if we had tied the whole bag of them to a ton of concrete and dumped it in the ocean.

Best of all, it means to me that my own dying, and yours too, will be undone. The story will not end in tears and despair, but with measureless and everlasting joy.

Years ago I stood in an Indiana cemetery on a day of rain and wind and watched as my own mother was buried. I thought, as I listened to her pastor speak the ancient words of faith over her, what a momentous thing we believe in the face of our dying. What a wondrous claim we make in the creed when we confess these words, that once there was a man who was as dead and cold as my mother in front of me in that casket, that his grave, too, was sealed shut, and his family and friends went home with heavy hearts, but the third day he came alive again.

Because he did, Forest Lawn Cemetery in Greenwood, Indiana, and every other quiet resting place will one day rustle and shudder and come to life. The very word "cemetery" says so, for it means "the place of those who sleep." At the call of Jesus Christ, the sleepers will waken and their bodies will be changed in a moment, in the twinkling of an eye.

We do not believe that the dead are simply annihilated, blown out like candles.

We do not believe in reincarnation, that people must go round and round in a dreary succession of lives as if trapped in a revolving door. The Bible says, "Man is destined to die once" (Heb 9:27), and after that comes not reincarnation, but resurrection. It is not some dreadful karma that powers the life to come, not the frightful chains of "what goes around, comes around," but that most liberating Gospel. Because of Jesus, our sins are forgiven, and we have passed from death to life.

Jesus rose in his flesh, and so shall we.

More than 200 years ago, a man named Samuel Medley got his chance to answer the question that high school girl read on her card. His answer? Listen to the words of the hymn he wrote: "He lives and grants me daily breath. He lives and I shall conquer death. He lives my mansion to prepare. He lives to bring me safely there."

He Lives. What fantastic news! What staggering implications for life! For some, like Samuel Medley, Easter is the beautiful music that carries them through their darkest days. For others, Easter is just another day on the calendar, and this news means nothing. What makes the difference?

Let me illustrate. Imagine yourself in a room at home. All is quiet. Too quiet. You flick the switch of an FM station, and in an instant, the room is filled with music. A concert is being broadcast live from the Kennedy Center

Creed Sermon Seven – "I Believe He Rose from the Dead"

in Washington, DC. It is the New York Philharmonic, playing Beethoven's majestic Ninth Symphony. But after a few moments, you decide you are not in the mood to listen, and you reach out a hand to switch it off. Again there is silence in the room. Has the music stopped?

Not at all. The music goes on. The orchestra at the Kennedy Center keeps on playing. But you cannot hear it now, for you are not tuned in. Beethoven's Ninth is still in the air all around you, but you are wrapped in silence because you turned the radio off.

It is Easter Day. Once again the music plays. Is Jesus Christ truly present? Is he alive, available with his grace and power? Indeed he is. But only those who are "tuned in" by faith can hear the music.

This phrase, like all the others in the creed, is finally an article of faith. Yes, there is "evidence" for those who are open to it, reasonable historical evidence that his grave was empty, a fact never seriously disputed, even by his enemies. Yes, God has surrounded us with innumerable hints of the resurrection in nature, such as the rebirth of a dead winter landscape into verdant blooming plants each spring, and the miraculous metamorphosis of caterpillar into butterfly within its tomb-like chrysalis.

And who can explain the phenomenal growth of the early church, a movement that would never have gotten off the ground had Jesus' followers not been convinced that he was alive?

Hints and evidence aplenty. But no final, conclusive proof. It is faith alone that hears the Easter music.

At the end of Mark's Gospel the Easter story comes to an end with surprising abruptness. The women come to the tomb, hear the angel's message, and run away like frightened rabbits. There the Gospel ends, and the reader is left hanging on the resurrection. That is what the church has been hanging onto for twenty centuries now, not on a conclusive set of proofs, but on the word of the angel and the promise of Christ.

It is what I call on you to hang on to today. Hang on, brother. Hang on, sister. Hang on to the news: Jesus rose again! He is alive. The symphony has begun. There will come a glorious finale: "On the Last Day, He will raise me and all the dead and give eternal life to me and all believers in Christ. This is most certainly true."[2]

Whatever you brought in here this morning—the guilt as you remember wasted opportunities, the chains of an evil habit that holds you fast, the

---

2. Luther, *Small Catechism*, 17.

despair of grief over some dear one you have lost, the fear of pain, of aging, of the relentless ticking of the clock—does not matter.

Hang it on the resurrection of Jesus, and let him have the last word. He is alive. He has removed the sins of *yesterday* and the uncertainties of *tomorrow* so that we may live triumphantly *today*.

Lift up your heads. Turn on the music. The third day he rose again from the dead!

And so shall we, for this is most certainly true.

Creed Sermon Eight – "I Believe in the Ascension"

A FAMILY WAS GATHERED one evening in the living room for family devotions. Father had just finished reading the story of our Lord's ascension when the youngest child piped up: "When Jesus finally got to heaven, God the Father told him, 'You better stay up here; otherwise, something will happen to you again!'"

Is that what this strange story of his ascension is all about—that Jesus has left the dangers of the world behind and is now safe in heaven?

Today as we continue our sermon series on the Apostles' Creed, we take a closer look at the portion which says: "He ascended into heaven and sits at the right hand of God the Father Almighty."

Let's face it. The festival of the Ascension isn't on most people's calendars. Nobody says "Happy Ascension Day!" Hallmark doesn't have an Ascension Day card section. Even in the church we don't do much with it. Among the holy days in the church year, Ascension Day gets only an honorable mention now and then.

That's too bad, because the Bible says a lot about the ascension, not only as a word about Christ, but also as a word about the church. Let's think about each one.

First, what are we saying about Christ when we confess these words? It sounds at first like we are saying, "Jesus is long gone, and we're left behind, all alone." That's likely how the eleven remaining disciples were feeling as he was parted from them that day. This was the end, a painful goodbye. We read in Acts chapter 1 that they stood there gazing into heaven.

We've done the same thing. Wives have watched husbands go off to war. Parents have watched children get married and move away. I recall vividly the day years ago when I stood near the runway at Portland Airport and watched as my wife and daughters flew off to Indiana. Like the disciples, I stood there "gazing into heaven" until the plane disappeared from sight. Then I drove home with a lump in my throat.

For the disciples, and for us, the message of the ascension sounds like the announcement of Christ's absence from our world. But is it? Jesus had promised them just the opposite: "I am with you always" (Matt 28:20).

When Paul writes of the ascension, he says that Jesus "ascended higher than all the heavens, in order to fill the whole universe" (Eph 4:10). In other words, Jesus' ascension did not result in his *absence* but in a completely new kind of *presence.*

Until that point, Jesus could be in only one place at a time. But from that day on, he could be everywhere at once, to hear, to heal, and to guide his church. He is not to be found sitting on a cloud or behind the moon. Instead he is now everywhere present, not only as God but also as man.

Let me illustrate. A circuit-riding evangelist of the nineteenth century rode his horse from one town to the next. He could be in only one place at a time. Given enough years, enough energy, and a sturdy horse, he could meet with thousands of people and share the Gospel. Today, a Gospel preacher can appear in hundreds or even thousands of homes in the very same hour, all because of the miracle of television.

In a greater way, the ascension is a miracle that makes possible the presence of Jesus in many places at once. Instead of being localized in Jerusalem, or Caracas, or Tallahassee, Jesus has come marvelously near to each of us. He is the unseen guest at every gathering in his name, and he is there residing in every believer's heart. Yours, yes? Mine too. That is the first meaning of Christ's ascension.

There is a second meaning that follows. The ascended Christ is not resting, nor hiding, as the child at that family devotion supposed. Rather, he is working in the world through his church.

The very first verse of Acts points this out in a quiet, but remarkable way. It says, "In the first book, O Theophilus, I have dealt with all that Jesus began to do and teach until the day He was taken up" (Acts 1:1–2).

Began? If he has only begun, then there must be more to come. His great saving work is "to be continued." As you read the Book of Acts, you see that it is. That book seems poorly named, for it is not so much the "Acts of the Apostles" as it is the "Acts of the risen and ascended Lord" himself, continuing his work on a grander scale, a worldwide stage.

But what work? What is this ascended Lord doing? The next phrase that follows in the creed explains. We confess that he "sits on the right hand

Creed Sermon Eight – "I Believe in the Ascension"

of God the Father Almighty." That doesn't mean he's tired, that he's relaxing as we might in our easy chair after a hard day. To "sit at the right hand" is a special term that means "to rule."

He has entered into his proper work of being a king. God the Father has made Jesus his "right hand man" in ruling the universe. An old church hymn says, "See, He sits on yonder throne. Jesus rules the world alone."

It's an astonishing thing we confess. We believe that there is a *man* running the universe. Even more astonishing is that the Bible tells us that he rules the universe for the church's benefit. Ephesians 1 puts it this way: "And God placed all things under his feet and appointed him to be head over everything for the church" (Eph 1:22).

"For the church"? To us it rarely looks that way. In a world torn by war and civil unrest, the church often suffers. In Sierra Leone, Lutheran missionaries had to flee the country. In Iraq, Syria and Nigeria, churches have been burned and believers murdered by ISIS fighters. Here in the United States, the teaching and values of the church, especially traditional marriage, are being challenged like never before. Many people, seeking more "authentic" spirituality, are leaving institutional churches and seeking alternatives. Militant atheism is flexing its muscles.

Yet the message of the ascension is plain. Jesus Christ is Lord, and he rules. We cannot see clearly all that he is doing to re-direct his church and reform the hearts of his people for bringing the Gospel to a changing culture. It is as if we stood watching a tapestry being woven—but from the underside. We cannot discern the pattern from "down here," only the tangled threads beneath the frame. But Jesus is at God's right hand. He knows what he is doing, and one day we shall see clearly the design that he is executing.

Here's another picture. The growth of the kingdom of God is like a building under construction in some great city. As we walk past, we see great machines in the mud. We see the clutter of scaffolding. We hear banging and hammering and the shouts of unseen workers. Much of what is being built is hidden until the day the scaffolding comes down, the landscaping is finished, the workers go home, and the finished building stands gleaming in the sun. Then there is a grand opening and we go in and see it for ourselves. Right now, all we see is his scaffolding. But you may be sure that Christ is ruling. He is building his kingdom.

That's the first meaning of his "sitting at God's right hand." There's another. He is at God's right hand as a special friend who speaks to the Father for us. The Book of Hebrews calls him "the great High Priest who lives to make intercession" for us (Heb 7:25).

Have you ever heard of the "hot line"? In 1963, President Kennedy was furnished a "hot line," a red telephone linked directly to the Russian President in Moscow so that in a time of crisis, there would be no delay in communication and peacemaking.

That we have an Ascended Lord means we have a "hot line to heaven," a direct link to God, to the power that rules the entire created universe. Since all of this is true, what the angels told those eleven disciples must be repeated to us. Stop gazing and get going.

The angels had it right. This is not a time for us in the church to stand and stare at the world, scratching our heads and wondering "what's up with that?" It is time to act. You and I have not been deserted. We have been empowered. So get ready, get set, go into all the world!

And as you go, don't lose heart. The ascension of Jesus means we need not panic about what we see happening in the church or our personal lives. The writer of Hebrews encourages us, "Since we have a great high priest who has gone through the heavens . . . let us hold firmly" (Heb 4:14). Jesus is risen. He has ascended into heaven. He has promised always to be with us, and that nothing will separate us from him. So we live with courage. And we bear our witness without fear.

On the dresser in my bedroom in my boyhood years was a little picture I had gotten from my Sunday school teacher. It was a picture of a boy on the deck of a ship, grasping the helm. The night was dark, and the ocean wild, but the boy's face was calm, for behind him stood Jesus, the great Captain, with one hand on the boy's shoulder and the other pointing ahead through the treacherous shoals.

We are not alone. Jesus lives, and he is present with us in every time of trial. We cannot see him, but by faith we sense his hand on our shoulder, calming our fears. Already our lives are hid with Christ in God. Already we sit with him in the heavenly places by faith (Eph 2:6). Already he is preparing a place for us.

Paul wrote to the Colossians: "When Christ, who is your life, appears, then you also will appear with him in glory" (Col 3:4). Until then, may the ascended Lord empower us to do what needs doing, not to gaze, but to go, not in panic but with good courage, for he who died upon the cross, and rose to life at Easter has "ascended into heaven and sits on the right hand of God the Father Almighty."

Creed Sermon Nine – "I Believe in Judgment Day"

Hang on tight for a sobering announcement: "The world is coming to an end!" Christians have always believed that, but these days, even the most hardened unbeliever would admit that the end of the world—or at least the end of civilization—seems a certainty.

Scientists speak of the death of the sun. Or a super collision with a giant asteroid. Or a new ice age descending. Such things, of course, don't bother most folks because the scientists add that none of this is likely for thousands or even millions of years. We grow more anxious, however, at the prospect of thermonuclear annihilation at the hands of some rogue terror-loving nation like North Korea or Iran. There are movies which picture a dreadful apocalypse where a few desperate survivors roam a desolated landscape.

Even the most stubborn skeptic will admit that the world *can* end. We Christians confess that it *will* end. But the end will not be brought to pass by the launching of a missile or the explosion of the sun. The end of the world is to be ushered in by the coming of a person, the return of Jesus Christ in judgment. We confess it in the creed: "He shall come to judge the living and the dead."

The Second Coming of Christ on Judgment Day is one of the basics of the faith. The Book of Hebrews calls it part of the "foundation" (Heb 6:2). It is a double-edged doctrine, both frightening and comforting, for it addresses the meaning and destiny of every human life. Your life. Mine too.

As we have done in previous sermons, we begin by asking "What do these words mean?" What does it mean to say, "He shall come"? By these words, the church has always understood that Jesus Christ will, quite literally, return to earth. We have it on the authority of the angels, who promised the Apostles, "This same Jesus, who has been taken from you into heaven, will come back in the same way you have seen him go" (Acts 1:11). Yes, and we have it on the authority of Jesus himself, who promised, "I will come again and take you to be with me" (John 14:3).

His coming will be visible. "Every eye will see him," says John in the Book of Revelation. His coming will be sudden and unexpected. No one knows when, notwithstanding the Jehovah's Witnesses and other groups who make predictions. Jesus himself said it would be as unexpected as the coming of a thief. Some of you here this morning are old enough to remember the electrifying news that President Kennedy had been shot in Dallas, Texas. Even more remember the terrifying morning of the attack on the World Trade Center in New York.

Christ's coming will happen just as suddenly. Just as unexpectedly. The trumpet of Judgment Day will sound while some are driving down the expressway, while others gaze at a computer monitor, and still others stand at an open refrigerator.

The future of this planet and everyone on it is wrapped up in his coming. We do not expect a gradual lessening of tensions in the political realm. We do not expect that scientific and technological advances will finally overcome every disease and curb every evil impulse in the human heart.

No, Jesus said. Things will get worse, not better. This age will grow more dangerous and desperate, like the pangs of a woman in labor growing increasingly severe, until our Lord returns and his new age is born.

He is coming, says the creed, for a specific purpose: "to judge the living and the dead." The same Jesus who came as Savior will come back as our judge.

Imagine this scene. A talented young defense attorney represents a client charged with murder. He pulls out all the stops and uses all his skill to defend his client. There were extenuating circumstances, he tells the jury, and "reasonable doubts." In due course the jury retires to deliberate. The verdict, announced two days later, is "not guilty." With the trial ended, the lawyer, who is a committed Christian, speaks earnestly with his client and warns him to steer clear of evil ways and evil friends. "Turn your life over to God!"

Imagine that years pass, and that the same man is arraigned once more. Again the charge is murder. When he is brought into the courtroom, the defendant discovers, to his surprise, that the lawyer who defended him years ago is now the presiding judge! At the conclusion of the trial, the

Creed Sermon Nine – "I Believe in Judgment Day"

jury renders its verdict: "Guilty." The judge orders the man to stand for sentencing. Soberly he speaks these words: "At your first trial, I was your advocate. Today, I am your judge." Jesus Christ, the baby born at Bethlehem, the friend of sinners, will one day sit on the great white throne of judgment. Artists in the Middle Ages portrayed Him with a crown on His head, a globe in his hand, and a sword issuing from His mouth. The Savior will become the Judge!

And what will that judgment be like? The Bible describes it as a separation. Sheep will be separated from goats, wheat from weeds, good fish from bad. For some it will be a moment of inexpressible joy as they hear him say, "Come, you who are blessed by my father, take your inheritance... prepared for you." For others, it will be a moment of utter horror and ruin, for they will hear Him say, "Depart from me, you who are cursed, into the eternal fire" (Matt 25:34, 41).

On what basis will we be judged? The Book of Revelation tells us that on that day, books will be opened in which are recorded the deeds of each person's life (Rev 20:12). Like a defendant on the witness stand, each person will have to give an account of his life, down to every idle word.

Years ago, President Richard Nixon was on trial for the cover-up of the Watergate break-in. Things hung in the balance until the playing of the tape-recorded conversations in the oval office. The nation listened in as those talks, once secret, became public knowledge. President Nixon was guilty.

What you and I have done and said in secret is all recorded in God's book. One day the books will be opened, and we will be held accountable.

But what about faith, we ask. Are we not saved "by grace, through faith"? Indeed we are. But on Judgment Day, God will be looking for evidence of that faith. Was our professed faith genuine, or a sham?

There will be no hiding on that day. All of us will stand before the throne. "He shall come to judge the living and the dead," says the creed. You will be there. So will I.

This doctrine serves two purposes. First, it warns us to be ready. Keep watch, said Jesus. Be ready at all times. The sad truth is that many will not be. The parable of the five foolish maidens asleep at midnight (Matt 25:1–13) is a reminder that even some who claim to be Christians and know he is coming back will be caught unprepared.

Readiness begins with repentance. People who join Alcoholics Anonymous are required to make a "fearless and searching moral inventory" of their lives. So must we. "Repent!" shouted John the Baptist. Repentance is a complete change, a 180-degree turn of the whole life. God does not want you to be a 10 percent Christian. Have you heard of that kind? A 10 percent Christian is a Christian from the neck up, and a pagan from the neck down. One who says, "Lord, Lord," but will not do what God commands. Let each of us here this morning consider it well, for he shall come to judge.

There is no time to waste. A Sunday school teacher asked her class, "If you knew for sure that Jesus was coming tonight, what would you do?" "I would pray," said one student, "and then I would tell someone else."

Have you told anyone else about the Lord? If not, what are you waiting for? He too shall face the Judge one day. He too shall hear either "Come, you blessed of my father" or "Depart from me, you workers of iniquity." The way you treat that person and the things you say to that person will help him toward one destination or the other.

"He shall come to judge." It is a word of warning to look closely at ourselves and realize the urgency of telling others. But let it also be for you a word of comfort. For the Lord Jesus Christ before whom we shall stand in judgment is the same Jesus who bought us back with his blood. The Small Catechism summarizes: "Jesus Christ . . . has redeemed me, a lost and condemned person, purchased and won me from all sins, from death, and from the power of the devil; not with gold or silver, but with His holy, precious blood and with His innocent suffering and death."[1]

When He comes again, we need not cringe in fear. Instead, he says, "Lift up your heads, because your redemption is drawing near" (Luke 21:28).

This very day Jesus holds out his hands to us with pardon for sin and the power to serve him. We wait like that eager young woman with an engagement ring on her finger whose next meeting with her man will be their joyful wedding day.

So it is that we wait, watchful, ready, and even eager. We do not seek revenge on anyone, for he shall come to judge. When we see evil men triumph and good ones cast down, we do not complain that life is unfair, because one day he shall come to judge.

The magnificent mosque of St. Sophia in Istanbul was originally a Christian Church. When it was captured by Muslim invaders, the Christian symbols and writings were painted over. One day a visitor noticed, as he stood under the great dome, that in one place, a picture of the ascended

---

1. Luther, *Small Catechism*, 16.

Creed Sermon Nine – "I Believe in Judgment Day"

Christ with arms outstretched was showing through the covering paint. The man exclaimed, "He is coming back. You cannot blot him out!"

He is. He is coming back for you, my friend, and for me.

Come to him today as your Savior. Repent of your sins. Trust him and serve him with all your heart, and his coming will hold no fear for you. The Bible ends with this promise: "He who testifies to these things says, 'Yes, I am coming soon'" (Rev 21:20).

Amen. Come, Lord Jesus.

Creed Sermon Ten – "I Believe in the Holy Spirit"

Years ago there appeared a book with the intriguing title *The Half-Known God*. It was, in fact, a book about the Holy Spirit. Of the three persons of the Triune God, the Holy Spirit is the one we know least about. Even what we do know seems only half-used.

I preach today about the Holy Spirit, not only because "I believe in the Holy Spirit" is the next phrase to cover in our series on the Apostles' Creed, but even more because we need to know this "half-known God" and experience the life he is waiting to give us.

Is there any doubt that our church needs that life? I'll put it more strongly. Our own church needs waking up, and many of us personally need reviving. Someone once labeled the Lutheran Church-Missouri Synod a "sleeping giant"—a church with great potential, a potential is too often unrealized in daily life. We are a church that seems to be sleeping through the harvest Jesus so urgently pointed out.

Is our own congregation sleeping too? Sleeping while some of our fellowship drift away from the Lord, sleeping while our children are seduced by a secular society, sleeping while the mission call of Jesus is forgotten or ignored? And which of us personally does not daily face the danger of relaxing our guard and letting the weeds that Satan plants choke the life and joy out of our faith? It is my prayer that the Holy Spirit will use this message to rouse some who are sleeping and to breathe a greater measure of life into our congregation.

First things first. Who is this "Holy Spirit"? The Greek word we translate as "spirit" can also mean "breath." Breathing is essential to human life. God breathed a breath of life into Adam's nostrils at the beginning. When Jesus imparts the Holy Spirit to the disciples in John 20, it is significant that he breathes on them. He had to breathe life into his trembling, impotent disciples before they could do anything useful.

Creed Sermon Ten – "I Believe in the Holy Spirit"

It is the Holy Spirit's job to give life to people who are dead in their sins, dead in their relationships, and dead in their imaginations. That's the reason the Nicene Creed calls him "the Lord and giver of life."

The Spirit was there moving over the face of the deep when God began his work of creation. He was there descending in the form of a dove when Christ began his ministry. He is there whenever a man or woman, boy or girl begins the new life in Holy Baptism. He is the life-giver at work!

Moreover, we call him the *Holy* Spirit because there are other spirits at work in the world. Some of you will remember reading about a woman named J. Z. Knight who began making appearances all over the country in the late 1980s. She claimed to channel a 35,000-year-old spirit named Ramtha. "Ramtha" promised listeners a secret philosophical wisdom for hundreds of dollars per session. Would you have gone? "Do not believe every spirit," writes John, "but test the spirits" (I John 4:1).

I preach about the Spirit given us by Jesus Christ on the Day of Pentecost. His coming was accompanied by the sound of a rushing, mighty wind. He breathed boldness into those trembling, cowardly disciples and they became a mighty apostolic band of witnesses.

That Spirit is still working. How does he give us life? Long ago Martin Luther summarized the work of the Holy Spirit with four verbs. In the Small Catechism, Luther wrote that he "calls, gathers, enlightens, and sanctifies the whole Christian Church on earth."[1]

First, he calls us. He must do so, for we would not come to God by our own choice. Indeed, we cannot, any more than we can give ourselves birth or raise ourselves from death. The catechism underlines our spiritual helplessness this way: "I believe that I cannot by my own reason or strength believe in Jesus Christ my Lord or come to Him"[2]

We are something like the wild animals who flee at the approach of humans. If humans want to get near those animals, or pet them, they cannot come stomping and shouting! No, they must come slowly, gently, with the offer of something good to eat.

So God comes to us in the midst of our fears, when we are primed to run away. He would win us into a relationship of trusting faith. He comes, not with threats and thunderclouds, but gently with the news of the Gospel, the sweet news that Jesus came to die for us and our sins are forgiven. That

---

1. Luther, *Small Catechism*, 17.
2. Luther, *Small Catechism*, 17.

assures us that he does not want to hurt us but to feed us and make us his dear children.

The irony of all this is that when the Holy Spirit is doing his proper work, we are not thinking about the Spirit at all, but about Jesus Christ. You might compare the role of the Holy Spirit with that of a book publisher. A publisher who is doing a good job does not hold his name before the public, but instead has them paying attention to the author and his book. The Holy Spirit is the publisher for Jesus Christ. By the Gospel he calls them to listen to Jesus and follow him. Have you heard him calling *you* to follow Jesus as Savior?

Those the Spirit calls, he also gathers. Paul describes that gathering process this way: "we were all baptized by one Spirit into one body …" (1 Cor 12:13). What Paul makes clear is that there are no "Lone Ranger Christians." There is no such thing as a true Christian who wants nothing to do with other Christians, who avoids public worship and sidesteps Holy Communion. Where the Holy Spirit is at work, God's people are not *scattered*, they are *gathered*.

If you hear a person say, "I can be a Christian without the church," you may be sure that the spirit at work in him is not the Holy Spirit. The life God's Spirit gives is not some private spiritual high, but the fellowship of the body of believers who love one another, encourage one another, admonish one another, and pray for one another.

That is why, in the creed, the words "I believe in the Holy Spirit" are followed immediately by "the Holy Christian Church." Is the Holy Spirit gathering us? Do we find ourselves being pulled closer together—into a deeper fellowship, a more serious study of the Word together, a more joyful service side by side?

The Holy Spirit is busy gathering the church. And those he gathers, he also enlightens. He turns on the lights of our hearts and minds. He helps us see and understand what we could make no sense of before.

Having information is not enough. Some of the most hardened unbelievers are people who know a great deal of information about God, the Bible, and the church, but who cannot see the meaning of it and will not live by it.

Even the disciples had this problem. "The Son of Man must suffer many things" (Luke 9:22) he told them, but they did not understand. "On the third day He will rise again" (Luke 18:44) he promised them, but after his crucifixion they sat shrouded in hopeless gloom. Their cause might

Creed Sermon Ten – "I Believe in the Holy Spirit"

have been hopeless and all Jesus' teaching in vain, had it not been for the Holy Spirit.

The Spirit "will remind you of everything I have said" (John 14:26) was Jesus' promise. And so it happened. The Holy Spirit helped them remember. Have you had a moment when the "lights finally went on"? When an old story or Bible verse or hymn or conversation long shelved in the back of your mind is finally lit up and you see it, as if for the first time?

The Holy Spirit enlightens us also by giving us special gifts: wisdom and knowledge and faith, hospitality, mercy, generosity, healing, teaching, and helpfulness. With such gifts, and others, he brings a shine to your life and power to serve. Have you discovered your gift? Are you using it?

Finally, he whom the Holy Spirit enlightens, he also sanctifies. To "sanctify" means to "make holy." God has lofty plans for us, not only to impart his life to us, but more and more to make us holy people whose lives are set apart for him. To make holy people out of unholy ones, he must finally come to dwell inside us and take up residence in each heart so that he may change our habits and cleanse our mouths.

The good news, my friend, is that he has already moved in to take up his dwelling. His move-in day was at your baptism. "Do you not know," writes Paul, "that your body is a temple of the Holy Spirit, who is in you, whom you have received from God?" (1 Cor 6:19).

The question is, what will you do now with that temple of yours? Will you use your body for sin, and so grieve the Holy Spirit that he must finally depart? Or will you honor his presence, listen to his voice, and bear fruit? For that is the Holy Spirit's goal for your life – the fruit which is love, joy, peace, patience, kindness, goodness, faithfulness, gentleness, and self-control.

Can you see it happening here? Do you see increasing devotion to Jesus Christ, a stronger determination to serve others, unquenchable joy even in the midst of trials, and a growing kindness to children, to the elderly, to the burdened and grieving?

Years ago, I stood looking at an incubator at a county fair. Rows of eggs in trays sat warming under a heat lamp. Here and there little cracks were appearing as tiny beaks worked the shells from inside. New life was hatching. It is happening here. And well it should, for we believe in the Holy Spirit.

May he gather us ever more closely, warm us with the promises of Christ, and empower us to serve him.

Creed Sermon Eleven – "I Believe in the Church"

If I say "church," what do you picture? A building with a steeple and stained-glass windows? Or perhaps an organization like our denomination with its headquarters in St. Louis, its own publishing house, and a network of colleges and seminaries? Is that the church?

Well, yes. And no. Yes, we often mean those things when we say the word "church," but we know that even if the organization disbanded and even if all the church buildings burned to the ground, there would still be "the Holy Christian Church."

For the church is people, all those people who know and follow Jesus Christ. Martin Luther commented that even a small child knows what the church is—sheep who hear the voice of their Shepherd.[1]

This truth was powerfully underlined a few decades ago when reports began filtering out of mainland China that Christianity there was alive and flourishing. Conservative estimates at the time placed the number of Christians in China at more than ninety million people, in spite of the fact that for many years under the Communist government there were few Bibles, church buildings were confiscated, and there was no external church organization. Nevertheless, the church was there. Even in the darkest days, there were people who heard the voice of Jesus, their Shepherd.

It will always be so. There are, and always will be, people who know and believe in Jesus Christ. That is what we confess with confidence when we say the words in the Apostles' Creed: "I believe ... in the holy Christian Church, the communion of saints."

But why is this in the creed? It takes faith to believe in God, certainly, for no one can see him. But everyone can see the church, can't they? Yes, and that's just the problem, some people say. We can see that there is a church all right, but is it really what you Christians claim it to be in your

---

1. *Book of Concord* (SA XII 2), 315.

Creed Sermon Eleven – "I Believe in the Church"

creed? Is it really holy? Are you really a "communion of saints" or simply a fellowship of fools who have deceived yourselves?

All around us we hear the church criticized or even dismissed. The sermons are boring, they say. The liturgy is irrelevant to our daily life. There are hypocrites in attendance. Some of the hypocrites are the clergy themselves, caught up in unbelievable scandals. Even worse, according to many, the church spends most of its time and energy on itself rather than caring for the poor and the discouraged. Add to that the observation that the church is hopelessly divided, and the picture seems gloomy in the extreme.

It takes faith to believe in the "holy Christian Church" these days. Sometimes, even we who are part of the church and love it have our doubts about it. We are stung by the criticisms, for we can see the church's faults and frailty, and we fear for its future.

In light of all that, I invite you to listen to the words of the creed more carefully. When we say I believe in the holy Christian Church, we are affirming four important things.

First, we are saying that the church is one and not many. "Church" is singular, not plural. It takes faith to say we believe in one church, because what we see all around us is multiplicity and division. Like a lovely vase dropped onto a concrete floor, the church has been shattered into literally hundreds of denominational pieces. They include Methodists, Mennonites and Moravians, Presbyterians, Dunkers, and Seventh-day Adventists, Shakers and Quakers, and half a dozen different kinds of Lutherans here in the USA.

There has always been outward division in the church. St. Paul had to admonish the Corinthians about factions right at the start, and it remains problematic today. As one hymn says it, the church is "sore oppressed, by schisms rent asunder, by heresies distressed."

Where then is the oneness? Ah, it lies where it always has—in Jesus Christ. All who genuinely believe in him are one, regardless of their denomination. There is only one church because there is only "one Lord, one faith, one baptism" (Eph 4:5).

The Bible uses pictures to express this. It says the church is a temple with Jesus as the foundation and we believers as living stones. It says the church is a living body with Jesus as the head and all us believers as the body's organs.

One evening a campus chaplain addressed a fraternity banquet. After his talk, during the question and answer period that followed, one student asked, "Chaplain, do you think the church will ever be one?" The chaplain replied, "It already is." While the chaplain was right in what he said, the student was also right to ask his question, because our behavior and our attitudes hide the church's unity and confuse people who watch.

If we confess that there is one holy Christian Church, that confession challenges us to work together as we do on the community food pantry, and to pray for each other, as our community's pastors do every month, and so work to overcome the things that still divide us. What are you doing personally in response to the prayer Jesus prayed: "that all of them may be one … so that the world may believe" (John 17:21)?

The second thing we are affirming is that the church is holy. "I believe in the holy Christian Church," and the next phrase makes it even stronger: "the communion of saints." That too takes faith to say.

A holy church? Saints? The everyday reality is that the church is jammed to the gills with sinners. "You have members down there," one angry man said to me, "who go to church on Sunday and live like the devil the rest of the week." Some of the saddest headlines are made by the clergy. A Lutheran pastor in Missouri was arrested for the murder of his wife. Pedophile priests and monks are discovered in almost every major diocese of the Catholic Church. A Baptist clergyman stole thousands of dollars from the offerings at his church.

Jesus himself taught that the visible church is a mixed bag. There are hypocrites mingled with genuine believers in every congregation. "Wheat and tares" is how he described us, growing side by side in his field (Matt 13:24–30). Not until Judgment Day, when God separates the genuine disciples from the hypocrites, will there be a "pure" church. Until then, we rely on what Paul wrote Timothy, "The Lord knows them that are his" (2 Tim 2:19).

What troubles us who know our faith is real is that even in ourselves we see weakness, sin, and death at work! We have doubts. We give in to temptations. We think shocking thoughts and utter shocking words.

The holiness of the church is not something we bring in through the door, but rather a gift God gives us here through his word of grace and pardon. I heard someone say it with a vivid picture: "The church is not a country club for saints, but a hospital for sinners." Yes, the church must be composed of sinners, for there are only two kinds of people in the world: sinners who are forgiven through Christ, and sinners who aren't.

Creed Sermon Eleven – "I Believe in the Church"

A saint, you see, is not a perfect person, but a sinner who has been "doctored" by the Holy Spirit and given the medicine of the Gospel. The "communion of saints" is the community of all those healed, cleansed, and dressed up in the new clothes of Jesus Christ. Hear how St. Paul says it in Ephesians 5: "Christ loved the church and gave himself up for her, to make her holy, cleansing her by the washing with water through the word, and to present her to himself as a radiant church . . . holy and blameless" (Eph 5:25–27).

Your holiness is a gift. Let that comfort you when you fail and fall. Let it move you to be gentle with others when they are weak. Let it challenge you to live a holier life in response.

The third great truth we confess in this phrase is that this one holy church is also catholic. That was the creed's original wording: "I believe in the holy catholic church." That word didn't mean the denomination we know as Roman Catholic. It meant "universal." To say the church is "catholic" means that it's inclusive of many different races and classes of people.

It takes faith to say that too, because we so rarely see beyond our own local congregation where almost everyone dresses alike, speaks English, and has the same color skin. Too often there is an exclusiveness about a congregation. Signs outside may announce "everyone welcome," but the attitudes inside often add "everyone like us, that is."

God had different plans. At Pentecost, he blew the doors open for people of every race and language to be one in Christ. Years ago, I caught a glimpse of the "catholicity" of the church at our church convention in St. Louis. There during the opening Communion service, I received the body of Christ from a black-skinned bishop from New Guinea, and the blood of Christ from a Chinese pastor with almond-shaped eyes. It was an unforgettable experience.

Today, of course, when we confess the creed, we do not say that good word "catholic" because we don't want to limit the church to a single denomination. Instead, we say "Christian." Even here, we must speak with care. For not every church that includes the name of Christ is truly Christian.

Paul warned the Galatians against those who would preach "another Gospel." So I urge you to test the spirits. If you move to a new place, test the churches. Listen carefully to what is preached and taught. Look for the presence of the living Christ among those who claim his name.

The Christian Church in which we believe is the church which stands in a line stretching back to the apostles. That's the fourth great truth. The church is apostolic. One. Holy. Catholic. Apostolic. The early believers "devoted themselves to the apostles' teaching" (Acts 2:42). So must we. That's what keeps the Church "Christian."

Think of it as a long bucket brigade. As communities long ago used to fight fires by handing buckets of water down the line, one to the next, so the church through the ages has stood in a long line, handing on that bucket with the precious water of life. Now it has reached us.

We are invited to take a long, deep drink from it, to hear and believe the message of Jesus for us and then to pass it on. It is our great joy to pass the bucket along, for it has satisfied us. It is also an urgent duty, for the church is always one generation away from extinction.

Let us not be content to *belong* to the church, like barnacles clinging to a pier. No, let us *be* the church—the holy Christian Church, the communion of saints, the people of God in Christ, as God has called us to be. Take the bucket, friend, and pass it on.

Creed Sermon Twelve –
"I Believe in the Life Everlasting"

THE APOSTLES' CREED COMES to an end with these soaring words: "I believe in . . . the resurrection of the body and the life everlasting."

A few years ago I boarded a United Airlines jet at O'Hare Airport in Chicago. The conference I had attended was over. I was tired and headachy, and my mind was absorbed with the pile of responsibilities that awaited me in my office the next morning.

I buckled myself in and waited. A few minutes later the plane lifted off into the night sky. I looked out the window and everything was transformed. There was a vast, shimmering network of lights—fixed grids of neighborhoods, dotted with shopping centers and schools, bisected by moving rivers of light that were expressways. Further away was the dark curve of Lake Michigan, and just this side of it the tiny circle of bright lights at Comiskey Park where the White Sox were playing a baseball game.

Have you had that view from above? Things are so different when seen from up there. For a time my headache was forgotten, and the work awaiting at home disappeared. I had a new look at life. I could see things normally hidden from sight when I'm earthbound.

We all need such moments. For the world closes in on us. Day follows day, and each brings new tasks and new burdens. We must go shopping, visit the dentist, write a report, remodel the kitchen, and pay the bills. The ultimate gets swallowed up by the immediate. We lose perspective—we forget who we are and where we're going.

A French priest named Michel Quoist wrote a book of prayers that put into words the thoughts I had on that plane. He said: "I would like to rise very high, Lord; above my city, above the world, above time. I would like to purify my glance and borrow your eyes."[1]

In this final sermon in this series on the Creed, let's look with God's eyes, see things from "up there" and get a vision of the life he offers. Let's think about these words: "I believe in … the life everlasting."

It's all about life. Our Lord once described his entire mission this way: "I have come that they may have life, and have it to the full" (John 10:10). By that Jesus means to tell us that real life, a full and abundant life, is more than having a pulse and brain waves, more than taking up space down here for 80 years or so, more than having all the stuff people think is so important.

I heard an old story about a rich Texan who died and was buried with an extravagant funeral service. As a finishing touch, he was lowered into an oversize grave—not in a casket, but in a pink Cadillac. Upon seeing this, one observer leaned over to another and said, "Man, that's really living!"

Sometimes we say the same about other people. We envy those who seem to have it all, the cars and the clothes and the money and the tan they got in Hawaii. They're "really living," we like to say. But are they? Or are they just dead people propped in a Cadillac?

Our Lord has a completely different life for us. A life that goes deeper, and lasts longer, even when health and money run out. So the creed adds an adjective. It is not merely "life" he offers us, but rather "life everlasting." This is the life the rich, young ruler was after when he came to Jesus and asked, "What must I do to inherit eternal life?" (Luke 10:25).

Our church body produced a long-running TV show many years ago. It was entitled *This is the Life*. And what sort of life is it? At the very least, this is a life that will not be ended by death. A life that goes on after this life ends.

Several years ago a best-selling book appeared with the title *Life after Life*. The author, Doctor Raymond Moody, assembled evidence from the testimonies of people who had gone through near death experiences and lived to share them. They described a life on the other side of death and the indescribable joy of being in the presence of a being of light. Most were sorry that they had to come back!

An astonishing book it was, but not really surprising to us who have taken seriously God's promise of a life on the other side of death.

---

1. Quoist, *Prayers*, 13.

Creed Sermon Twelve – "I Believe in the Life Everlasting"

People are curious about it. Now and then someone will ask, "What is heaven going to be like? Will we be playing harps? Singing? Attending a never-ending church service? Will it be boring?"

The New Testament answers our questions by affirming two things about life everlasting. First, we shall be *with* Christ. Remember how Jesus comforted the thief on the cross beside him? "Today you will be with me in Paradise" (Luke 23:43). When St. Paul sat in a jail cell facing his own death, he wrote of his hope: "I desire to depart and be with Christ" (Phil 1:23).

To be with our Savior. To see his wonderful face. Nothing boring about that! The sweethearts walking hand in hand aren't bored. They're thrilled. And how about the music lovers at the concert of their dreams? They're not bored. They're pulsing with the rhythm, their bodies keeping time.

It will be that way for us too. St. Paul captures the wonder of it in 1 Corinthians 2:9: "No eye has seen, no ear has heard, no mind has conceived what God has prepared for those who love him."

What's more, the Bible tells us, we shall not only be with Christ. We shall be *like* Him. Like him, in part, because we shall share in his resurrection. The miracle of Easter shall be repeated in you and me. We shall, at the last day, be gathered from our graves to live again. "I believe in the resurrection of the flesh" was the original wording of the creed.

The flesh. This poor "sack of worms" (as Luther once called it)[2] will somehow be transformed into a new and glorious body. All tears wiped away. Death itself swallowed up. We shall also be like him by sharing his work—judging the angels, ruling the new heavens and the new earth at his side. Not sitting on clouds like celestial couch potatoes, but sitting on thrones as co-rulers with Christ!

Randy Alcorn wrote a book entitled *Heaven* about that life to come. He says it is a common mistake to spiritualize the eternal kingdom of God. He explains that as surely as Adam and Eve ruled Eden, so we will rule in the new world God will unveil.[3]

If you think all this sounds rather fantastic and other-worldly, if it sounds to you like a lot of "pie in the sky by and by," I have saved the best till last. The great good news is that everlasting life begins right here, right now.

Will you look at your bulletin, at the verse written there right under the sermon title? "I tell you the truth, he who believes has everlasting life" (John 6:47). He does not say *might* have it if you hang on long enough. He

---

2. Kurz, *Being Lutheran Matters*, par. 16.
3. Alcorn, *Heaven*, 207.

does not say *will* have it some day when you die. He says "has." Present tense.

Indeed, for most of us, eternal life has already begun. The plane has not yet headed down the runway, but we are on board, buckled in, and we can feel the engines revving. Already we have been plunged into this new life at our baptism. Already we have experienced that sweet forgiveness, for the Savior has pulled away our sins like the workers who pull the chocks from the jetliner's wheels.

Already, because of Jesus, we have the "peace that passes understanding," even in the midst of the daily grind, even in the emergency room and the nursing home. Even in the midst of fears and frustrations and depression, we have a hold on that life because he has a hold on us. It has begun, but we cannot see it clearly yet.

When our children were small, we took a trip for our first look at Crater Lake in southern Oregon. We were excited. When we arrived, however, our spirits sank because everything was fog-bound. The signs on the road said "Viewpoint," but all we could see was the gravel road and some scrubby fir trees. All else was shrouded by a thick blanket of white. We knew the lake was there. The map said so. The signs said so. But we could not see it with our eyes. We waited for ten minutes, then fifteen, growing more discouraged.

Just as we were about to drive away, a breeze rose and the fog parted. There before us was a sight beyond even what we had hoped. We were high up on the wall of the ancient crater. Hundreds of feet below us was the lake—a brilliant beautiful blue—and jutting out from it was Wizard Island, with the tiny tour boat circling. I thought to myself, "What if I had simply driven down this road without a map or road signs? Without knowing the unseen lake was there? I would never have stopped, let alone waited. And we would never have seen what we saw that day."

It's like that with the life God gives. The Scriptures like a sure and certain map point out the life everlasting. The preachers are the road signs that alert us, "you're getting closer." But even when we stand within the very park boundaries, at the very cliff edge, there are times when the fog rolls in and we see nothing. We are surrounded by the haze of chemotherapy, numbed by the pain of family conflict, blinded by the blur of an over-crowded schedule, and we see nothing. "It is near," God says, but its beauties are unseen, and largely forgotten as we pass our days and years.

Creed Sermon Twelve – "I Believe in the Life Everlasting"

Have faith, dear people. Faith in God, faith in the promises he makes to us in Christ. "God so loved the world that He gave His one and only Son, that whoever believes in him shall not perish, but have eternal life" (John 3:16).

That's where it begins—wherever people know God and trust what he tells them. Do you know him? Have you trusted what he tells you? Then don't be afraid. One day the fog will lift. Or shall I rather say, one day God will lift us up out of the fog, from the meanness and the warfare and this veil of tears. We shall rise very high—above our city, above our world, above time itself. Then *faith* will turn to *sight* and we shall see him as he is.

The Small Catechism announces what we so gloriously anticipate: "On the last day He will raise me and all the dead, and give eternal life to me and all believers in Christ. This is most certainly true."[4]

That is the Apostles' Creed, from start to finish. That is the glorious summary of the faith once delivered to the saints, and now passed to us. Let us stand and confess our faith together with them.

---

4. Luther, *Small Catechism*, 17.

The Lord's Prayer

Lord's Prayer Introduction – "Calling God 'Father'"

OUR LORD JESUS BEGAN his master lesson on prayer with these words: "And when you pray, do not keep on babbling like pagans, for they think they will be heard because of their many words. Do not be like them, for your Father knows what you need before you ask him. This, then, is how you should pray: 'Our Father in heaven, hallowed be your name'" (Matt 6:7–9).

Can you remember the first time you prayed? Most of us cannot. For as long as we remember, we have been folding our hands and bowing our heads.

One of the earliest prayers we learned was the one we call the Lord's Prayer, the "Our Father." We heard it in church, a hundred voices speaking as one. We prayed it at home. Most of us memorized it long ago, maybe in German: "*Vater unser, der du bist im Himmel . . .*"

We know it so well and so deeply, that if one day our minds grow senile, it will be one of the last things to go. I've often seen that play out in nursing homes. There I visit older folks who cannot remember much nor speak clearly. But almost always, if I begin to pray the Lord's Prayer, they will join in.

It is a brief, easy prayer to pray, only seventy words long. Because we say it so often, we can say it almost in our sleep. And that is precisely the problem. It is an easy prayer to say, but a very difficult prayer to pray with real concentration. After having prayed it hundreds or even thousands of times, one finds the mind wandering!

Why do we go on praying it? Because our Lord Jesus himself put the words in our mouths. Luke tells us that Jesus taught this prayer in response to a request from one of the disciples: "Lord, teach us to pray" (Luke 11:1).

We are asking him too. For some of us have a prayer life that has grown weak and listless. With Paul we confess that we don't know how to pray as we ought. Some of us, I'm afraid, have given up believing that our praying makes any difference. We pray without conviction, just going through the motions. So you and I must say it too: "Lord, teach us to pray."

The goal of these messages on the Lord's Prayer is that we may learn again to pray with understanding and with the faith that we are heard and will be answered.

This morning, we begin at the beginning, with the very first words: "Our Father." That first word ought to jolt us. "Our"? How commonly we pray in the singular: "I want," "Give me." How different the Lord's Prayer would sound if we prayed it that way: "My father, who art in heaven … give me this day my daily bread, forgive me my trespasses . . . lead me . . . deliver me."

Instead, Jesus teaches us to say "us" and "our" so that we remember we are part of a larger family, a community of faith, people who share the same Father. We dare not pray for ourselves alone, like some impatient, selfish child who rushes to the family dinner table and begins gobbling food without waiting for anyone else. No. We say "us" and "our," for he has called us to love others as we love ourselves—to forgive them, feed them, to pray for them, and care for their souls' welfare as we care for our own. Until we are ready to treat one another as brothers and sisters, to pray this prayer in plural and not singular, we had better not pray this prayer at all!

But there's comfort in this word too. When we say "Our Father," we are reminded that we are not alone. We do not face life's alarms and tests by ourselves. Others pray with us, and for us. I once heard a speaker say, "Do you realize this prayer is being prayed at every moment by fellow Christians somewhere in this world? And that they are all lifting you up as they do?" Let that very first word, "our," comfort and uphold you with the reminder that you are not alone.

The second word is Father. We who are so familiar with this prayer find it a natural thing to call God "Father." But it wasn't always so. Jews in Jesus' day did not dare to put themselves on such intimate terms with a holy God. Their common form of address was "Lord," a term of respect something like our word "sir." But Jesus opened the door to a new and more daring way to pray: "When you pray, say 'Father.'" Many of the times we read of Jesus praying to the Father in the Gospels, he was not using the formal term "father" as we use it, but a word used by little children: *abba*, which is like our "Daddy"!

That speaks volumes about the God who hears our prayers. It tells us that he is a person, not a force, an idea, or a piece of machinery. Too many prayers are prayed as if God were a sort of vending machine. Say the right words, pull the right lever, and out pops whatever you want, just by going through the motions. How many prayers are prayed in the same way we leave messages with answering machines? "When you hear the tone, leave your message." One doesn't know if he'll hear back at all, and certainly is not expecting someone live at the other end! But if God is our Father, our prayers can no longer be the mechanical routines they often become. Instead, they become a conversation with a living person who is listening right now.

Nor is our Father a stranger. He knows us better than we know ourselves, for he made us. He knows what we mean, even though we cannot find the words. He knows what we need, even before we ask, as Jesus tells us.

Doesn't that help us begin to understand why it seems our prayers go unanswered, or are answered in a way different than we wanted or expected? For if God is really our father, then like any good father, he will not always give us what we *want*, but what we truly *need*.

You who are parents know the difference. You love your children, and you listen intently to them and to what they ask for, whether it is a cell phone, a motorcycle, a new puppy, or (as I once asked my father) a pellet rifle. If it seems wise, you give them what they ask.

But sometimes you will not, for they may be too young, too inexperienced to know what they need, or to realize what that might be dangerous for them to have just now. Even though they will not understand your refusal, and they might get angry with you, you say no. Trust God as your Father. "Your father knows what you need before you ask him," says Jesus (Matt 6:8). My dad, as I recall, waited a while before buying me the pellet rifle I'd wanted.

That word "Father" tells us not only about the God who is listening to our prayers. It tells us how we may feel as we come to him. He's encouraging us to come with affectionate trust and perfect confidence. Remember how the catechism puts it? "God tenderly invites us to believe that He is our true Father, and that we are His true children, so that with all boldness and confidence we may ask Him as dear children ask their dear father."[1]

But isn't that exactly where it becomes hard to pray this way? For not all of us had "dear" fathers. Some of us had fathers who were always gone— at work, or at a game, or with their buddies, or God only knew where. Some

---

1. Luther, *Small Catechism*, 19.

of us had fathers who were alcoholics, or cursed at our mothers or slapped us kids around.

And how can any of us pray "Our Father" in a world that seems, at times, to be utterly fatherless, a world where war devastates and diseases cripple and broken-hearted children are orphaned?

In our own strength we cannot pray this prayer. We can pray it only as we remember the one who teaches us this prayer. Jesus came down from the Father. He entered this fatherless world, bringing the Father's love with Him.

German preacher Helmut Thielicke likens us to a frightened young soldier on sentry duty. He hears footsteps approaching in the dark, and he wonders if this is a friend or an enemy. "Who goes there?" he shouts.[2] And so might we, if left alone. Without a Savior, that's how the world looks to people. There is Something out there, Something that fills us with dread. How can one pray to "something" like that?

But that "Something" is a "Someone" and no longer a mystery. Jesus has come to us, and the wondering and fear are ended. "The Father sent me," he assures us. It is the Father waiting on tiptoe to welcome the prodigal, the Father with open arms and a bursting heart, the one to whom Jesus Himself prayed on the cross, "Father, into your hands I commit my spirit" (Luke 23:46).

The arms of Jesus embrace us from the cross. His strong voice, alive again from death, calms our hearts. We pray with perfect confidence, for we know we have a Father. For a time, we must all journey toward that Father in the darkness of this world. But it's different now, with our Savior by our side. We do not walk alone. We do not pray into a void. God is there. He is listening. And he will answer. One day faith will give way to sight, and we will say with joy as we see him, "Oh Father, our Father!"

---

2. Thielicke, *Our Heavenly Father*, 30.

The First Petition: "Hallowed be Your Name"

Jesus said, "This . . . is how you should pray ... hallowed be your name" (Matt 6:9).

We are surrounded by names. Cell phone contact lists bulge with them. Billboards are plastered over with them. Television commercials drone them into our ears. Smith and Jones, Washington and Lincoln, Yankees and Dodgers, Bach and Beethoven, Ford and Chevy and Toyota, Budweiser, Miller, and Coors. So many names in our heads, and on our lips!

Names are important. Years ago, people called them handles, a good description of how names function. If I know your name, I have a handle on you. I can call out "Jim!" or "Tracy!" and almost literally spin you around. I can get in touch with you, bless you or curse you, if I know your name.

Among all those hundreds and thousands of names, how important is the name of God to us?

When Jesus was teaching his disciples how to pray, he made this the very first petition: "Hallowed be your name." If Jesus had not taught us to start here, how many of us would ever bother to pray about the name of God? Would we not simply begin with our own needs?

The modern church has suffered a loss of reverence for God's name. We say the name of God so easily, so thoughtlessly. We must stop and ask why our Lord begins here. What is he having us pray for when we say "Hallowed be your name"?

The dictionary says that "hallow" means "to make holy," or "to honor as sacred." Luther's Small Catechism explains it this way: "God's name is certainly holy in itself, but we pray in this petition that it may be kept holy among us also."[1] To hallow is to make holy. That's a place to start.

In our world, however, even the word holy is misunderstood. People think of monasteries, burning candles, and haloes. But we don't live in a

---

1. Luther, *Small Catechism*, 19.

monastery. So how are we to go about treating God's name in a holy way sitting at the computer in a cubicle, or walking through the cafeteria line at school, or watching football with friends?

The word "holy" means "set apart for special use." To hallow God's name, then, would mean that when using the name of God, we would always think of it as something important, and that we would use it for the purpose God intended when he gave it to us.

Is that what you hear when you listen to people using God's name? How often is it used to "damn" this or that? How often is it a thoughtless reaction to some news, however trivial, as people say "Oh, my God"? One day a pastor entered an elevator on his way to the top of an apartment building to visit some shut-in members of his church. On the way up, he listened to two older women talking. Over and over he heard "Oh, my God." Finally, he couldn't stand it anymore. "I wish you wouldn't use God's name like that" he told one of them. She looked genuinely apologetic. "I'm sorry," she said, "I didn't mean anything by it."

Not to mean anything when you say "God" is just the problem! How can we use such an important word and not mean anything by it? Doing that vulgarizes it, cheapens it so that finally the name of God is just another word.

So important is this to God that he made it one of his Ten Commandments: "You shall not take the name of the Lord your God in vain," that is to say for no purpose. He even adds this threat: "The Lord will not hold him guiltless who takes his name in vain" (Exod 20:7 RSV).

But it's more than just a matter of words. God's name can be hallowed or desecrated by our deeds as well. The truth is that we who call ourselves Christians not only speak the name of God. We carry it around with us. We wear it for all to see. Our neighbors and co-workers and classmates are watching to see how people who wear God's name will act.

A young man was about to leave home for the first time and go away to college. His parents accompanied him to the train station, where the father placed his hand on the boy's shoulder. "Son," he said, "you'll be on your own at college, and I won't be telling you what to do or not to do any more. I just ask you to remember one thing. Remember what name you carry, and bring honor to it."

This name—the name of God, and of Jesus Christ—is the name we carry. God gave us this name when we were baptized. It's our identification card. It identifies us as his people, his family. Can you imagine what

The First Petition: "Hallowed be Your Name"

happens to God's reputation among people when those who wear his name are seen by others to be drunkards and slanderers, adulterers, and liars? Are God's people greedy, grouchy, joyless folks? Are they lazy couch potatoes?

One of the biggest reasons people reject Jesus Christ is that they are turned off by the way people who wear Jesus' name are acting. We cannot pray this petition sincerely without confessing how often we ourselves have misused and betrayed his holy name by unholy living and unholy talking

If we think further, we will remember moments when we failed to use it the right way—when we could have spoken out with joy about how good he had been to us or offered the help he might bring others, but we didn't.

We remember such moments this morning as we come into his presence. How can we face him? Ah, because the name he commands us to hallow and respect is the very same name he promises to use for our help and healing.

We can come into the Father's presence because of a name—the holy name of Jesus. This same Jesus who teaches us to say "Hallowed be thy name" is the one who shed his blood to cleanse foul mouths and rose again to redeem phonies and hypocrites to live a new way, with new lives that honor God's name.

Do you want to hallow God's name? Then begin today by confessing what you have done with his name this week. Don't be afraid. That's one of the reasons he gave us his name: "Call upon me in the day of trouble; I will deliver you, and you will honor me" (Ps 50:15).

Think of his name as his business card, a way to reach him and to ask for what you need. In the children's choir room in one Lutheran church there is a poster with the names of Jesus on it. Week by week, their director is teaching the children to use those names to call on God in prayer. The children are learning about that beautiful, valuable business card.

You can use it, too, to pray, praise, and give thanks. Use that name to pray for strength so that more and more we are occupied not with our own reputations but with his. Use that name to praise God or give thanks the next time a store clerk says "So how are you today?"

Let me hold before you a vision. In the Book of Revelation, John sees the saints standing on Mt. Zion. They had the Lamb's name and the Father's name written on their foreheads (Rev 14:1). By the grace of Jesus, you and I are in that picture! His name is on our foreheads, placed there in our baptism. Doesn't it make you want to live and speak differently?

An old story tells how the legendary general Alexander the Great was walking among his troops. As he did so, he met a slovenly, ill-mannered soldier under his command. "What is your name?" barked the general. "Alexander," the soldier replied carelessly. The general's eyes widened. "Alexander? Well, then, you must either change your name, or change your ways!"

By the grace of Jesus, we carry God's own name. Let us pray this petition thoughtfully, so that tomorrow morning, as we begin our day at school, at work, or at home, we remember whose name we bear and hallow it by the way we live.

The Second Petition: "Your Kingdom Come"

During these Sundays, we come to our Lord asking: "Lord, teach us to pray." Today, we hear Him say, "This ... is how you should pray . . . your kingdom come" (Matt 6:9–10).

When we pray this second petition of the Lord's Prayer, we feel as if we are stepping into the past, for kings and kingdoms have largely disappeared. We've read about the old kings of the past century that have fallen one by one. Czar Nicholas of Russia, Emperor Haile Selassie of Ethiopia, and the Shah of Iran are all long gone. The old royal palaces in Leningrad and Versailles have become tourist attractions. A few kings still rule, mostly in the Middle East. But in most countries where they still exist, like Great Britain, kings and queens are largely figurehead rulers, stripped of any real power.

So what sense does it make these days to pray about a kingdom? Where is this kingdom for which we pray?

We must begin by saying where this kingdom is not. The kingdom of God is not any particular country. We Americans like to speak as if the United States were that kingdom, the world's foremost Christian nation, a kind of new Israel. In reality, the United States has become a largely post-Christian nation. Some guess there will soon be more Christians in Africa than in North America.

The kingdom of God doesn't have a mailbox in St. Louis or Chicago. I can't drop a letter in the box or send an e-mail addressed "kingdom of God" and hope it will be delivered because, as Jesus made clear long ago, God's kingdom isn't a place.

Well, then, if it isn't a place at some identifiable address, where are we to find it? Here is the answer: a kingdom exists wherever a king is ruling. That's how it works in a game of chess. It doesn't matter how many pieces a player has left on the board. If he still has his king which hasn't been checkmated, he is still in the game. He still has a kingdom!

Wherever God is ruling as King, there is the kingdom of God. Several writers have suggested that if the word "kingdom" makes us think chiefly of a place, we would do better to use the word "kingship." What we are praying about here is that God might rule in this world—that he might exercise his kingship over people.

Ah, but when will that happen? It certainly doesn't look as if God were ruling much of anything just now. The police are increasingly targeted and ambushed. There is often open warfare in the Middle East and lots of fear about the widening of such conflict. There is deadly pollution of our environment, religious and political strife everywhere, and the unrelenting collapse of many families.

One day the Pharisees asked Jesus when the kingdom would come. They had reason to wonder. The Romans ruled with an iron fist. King Herod acted like a madman, murdering his wife and children. Taxes were exorbitant, and many tax collectors were cheats. There was a floodtide of poor and sick people, and the city of Jerusalem had lost her former glory.

"When is God's kingdom coming?" they asked, and we look searchingly at Jesus too. When? When is God going to set things straight again? Luke records his answer: "The kingdom of God does not come with your careful observation, nor will people say, 'Here it is,' or 'There it is,' because the kingdom of God is within you" (Luke 17:20–21).

Jesus' answer to our anxious question when is that the kingdom of God has already come. It is here now. It stands among you, right in the middle of all of you, in the person of me!

It was an astonishing message. And all the more because Jesus did not look especially kingly. Like the Jews, we are impressed with wealth and power. These days we take note of hefty bank accounts, sophisticated weaponry, fast cars, and political clout. And here stands Jesus with none of that, daring to say that the kingdom of God has come and that he is the King!

Pilate couldn't believe it as he scrutinized the sorry-looking prisoner who stood before him with a crown of thorns pressed into his head and a tattered purple robe draped over his bleeding body. "Are you the king of the Jews?" he asked incredulously (Matt 27:11).

People today still have a hard time believing it, for the majesty of Jesus is still hidden under suffering and the cross and the ordinariness of the church. Jesus still takes his stand with the poor, the helpless, the little people, and those who follow him are made fun of as dreamers or dolts.

The Second Petition: "Your Kingdom Come"

That, of course, is just how he said it would be in his parables. The kingdom of heaven, Jesus explained, starts as a thing so tiny as to be invisible. It is yeast in a bowl of meal. It is seed growing secretly in a field. Yet it is there indeed, and nothing will stop its growing.

Well, then, why bother to pray this prayer at all? Why ask for the kingdom to come if it has already arrived before we pray? Listen to Martin Luther in the Small Catechism: "The kingdom of God certainly comes by itself without our prayer, but we pray in this petition that it may come to us also."[1] The question, you see, is not "Does Christ really rule as king?" but rather "Does he rule me? Is he *my* king?"

Writer C. S. Lewis invites us to understand "Your kingdom come" this way: "Enemy-occupied territory—that is what this world is. Christianity is the story of how the rightful king has landed, you might say landed in disguise, and is calling us all to take part in a great campaign of sabotage."[2]

Can you see that praying "your kingdom come" might turn out to be both a dangerous and difficult prayer? Dangerous, I say, because it is like joining on with that rightful king, signing up to serve in his army, and putting our lives on the line in the guerrilla warfare that is sure to follow. Yes, war! With all the hatred and viciousness that happens in any war. Difficult, I say, because down deep inside, none of us really wants to yield control of our lives to him. Things feel much safer, more predictable, if we can run our own lives.

If we pray this prayer, we will be asking the King to take over full control of our lives. Are we ready for that? For it will mean he takes control not only of the Sunday-go-to-church part of us, but the whole Monday thru Saturday part too. It will impact our conduct on the job, the spending of our money, our leisure time and hobbies, our sexual behavior, the way we treat our families, what we drink, what we watch. Everything!

It is our most terrible struggle—this call to abdicate our life's control room (the throne room) to him. That is why we pray this prayer, for without his help, we could not do it.

When we pray for his kingdom to come, we ask for the King to come to us, forgive us, and go to work with his Spirit turning us away from sinful habits, and turning us toward daily obedience. And he will, you know. That's why he went to the cross.

---

1. Luther, *Small Catechism*, 19.
2. Lewis, *Mere Christianity*, 51.

But that's only the beginning. For once we give this King our allegiance, he gives us the job of extending his kingship to other people. "Your kingdom come" means not only "Lord, let your kingdom come *to* me" but also "Let your kingdom come *through* me." To my neighbors. And the people I work beside. The man who rides the bus into town with me. The woman behind the desk at the health club where I work out.

Think further, outside our community, our borders. Every day more than a million children are born. If things continue as they are now, many of those children will never even hear about Jesus, let alone believe in him.

Can you see how large a prayer this has become? We dare to pray such a large prayer and make such ambitious plans, because we have a great king! He went all the way into death and the grave for us. He came all the way back out on Easter morning, and all the way back up to heaven at his ascension. Though hidden now beneath the message of the cross, though hidden in the ordinary people of the church, one day everyone will see his majesty.

In the place where I live a large interstate highway bridge is being remodeled and earthquake-proofed. For two years the work has gone on, obscured by cranes, earth-movers, mounds of dirt, and traffic cones. When at last the cones and dirt are hauled away, the heavy equipment removed, the new paving completed, and the striping and lighting installed, we will get to see the bridge standing beautiful and strong as the engineers intended.

It will be that way with the kingdom of God. One day a million golden angel trumpets will sound their glorious blast, and the wraps will come off. Every eye will see that God has not been idle, that Jesus is not a figure in an old storybook, but a living, mighty King.

On that day every knee will bow, and every tongue confess that Jesus Christ is Lord: "He is the mighty King, Ruler of everything. His name is Wonderful, Jesus my Lord!"

Pray that that day will come soon, and that you and I and many more will be a part of it.

The Third Petition: "Your Will Be Done"

EACH WEEK WE ARE coming to our Lord Jesus, making the same request the disciples once made: "Lord, teach us to pray." Today we hear Him say, "This . . . is how you should pray ... your will be done on earth as it is in heaven" (Luke 6:9–10).

Of all the petitions in the Lord's Prayer, this one is surely the hardest for us to pray and really mean it. "Your will be done"? Even as we say it, we may feel that we are handing God a blank check—that we are allowing him to take us down some mysterious road whose end we cannot see.

It is hard enough to say "your will be done" on ordinary days, but how shall we say it when we are on the verge of being laid off, or watching helplessly as a loved one lies dying in the hospital?

We cannot pray this prayer freely, we say, because we do not know the will of God. "God works in a mysterious way" is how one old hymn puts it. And because his will is mysterious, we are afraid of what it may contain.

A woman was talking about it with her neighbor one day. "I don't dare pray, 'Your will be done,'" she said, "because I am afraid that God will take away my little boy or send some tragedy." The neighbor replied, "What would you do if your son came up to you tomorrow and said, 'Mom, I want to be and to do just what you want for me all day today'? Would you say, 'Ah, now's my chance to put the little fellow through some real misery'?" "Surely not!" retorted the first woman. "I would try to plan the best day possible for him. I'm his mother!" "Well, then," said the neighbor, "why are you so afraid of God? Is he not your father?"

How easily we forget that God is our Father, not some celestial ogre waiting to rough us up. Just as that mother was sure her plans for her son would spring from her love for him, so do our Father's plans for us and for our world.

Nor is his will a mystery, as we often think. The Bible tells us clearly and often what he intends to accomplish in our lives. May I show you what I mean? Take a Bible from the rack in front of you and turn to 1 Timothy 2. Start reading at verse 1, where Paul instructs Timothy about prayer (read): "I urge, then, first of all, that requests, prayers, intercessions and thanksgiving be made for everyone—for kings and all those in authority, that we may live peaceful and quiet lives in all godliness and holiness. This is good, and pleases God our Savior, who wants all men to be saved and to come to a knowledge of the truth" (1 Tim 2:1–4).

Did you see what it is God wants, that is to say, his will? "God . . . wants all men to be saved and to come to a knowledge of the truth." Or back up a few pages to 1 Thessalonians 4, verse 3, where this same writer Paul says to a whole congregation: "It is God's will that you should be sanctified." In other words, he wants us to live a holy life. He goes on to mention avoiding sexual immorality as one particular.

No mystery here! God's will is that we come to faith in Jesus and be saved, and that as saved people we lead holy lives. The catechism adds that God's will happens "when He strengthens and keeps us firm in His Word and faith until we die."[1] That is God's will for every person here.

But if that is true, why do we see so much of what that young mother feared as we look around? Suffering. Disease and death. Unexplainable heartache. Even more disturbing is the fact that these things happen not only to people who thumb their noses at God but also to those who seek to know and do God's will in their lives.

We try to reason it out by asking why. If God really is in charge, then his will is being done, isn't it? Then everything that happens, including the freak accidents and malignant tumors, the warfare, the terrorism, the raping and robbing and devastation, must be his will too. Mustn't it?

Unless . . . unless there are other wills at work in this world! When our Lord Jesus came face to face with the agony of people, their crippled limbs and blinded eyes and broken hearts, did he say to them, "Calm down. This is all the will of God, so accept it"?

No. He recognized it for what it was, the work of an enemy. That enemy, he said, is busy sowing weeds in God's wheat field (Matt 24:24–30) and keeping many people bound in some infirmity. When we pray this petition, therefore, we are praying not only *for* the will of God, but *against* the will of the Devil, God's enemy and ours.

---

1. Luther, *Small Catechism*, 20.

The Third Petition: "Your Will Be Done"

But there's more. Satan would never get to first base if he did not have inside help. If you want to see one of your soul's great enemies, look in the mirror. Scripture tells us that it is our own evil desire that gives birth to sin. The Devil has an ally in our own sinful will.

Can we see why God must so often work in such mysterious ways to accomplish things in this world? Isn't it because at almost every turn, we ourselves oppose Him, saying, "Not your will but mine be done!"

God must use whatever means he can to rouse us from the selfish haze of our sin-addiction, to tear us away from those things—even those very good things—that might become idols. This petition, therefore, is a struggle in which we pray not only against the devil but also against ourselves. Unless we pray this prayer and mean it, how can the will of God ever be done in our lives? For by ourselves, it is clear, we cannot do God's will.

But we are not by ourselves. We are in the presence of the One who teaches us to pray this prayer. Jesus said he had come to do the Father's will. Most clearly of all he said it in Gethsemane: "Not my will but thine be done" (Luke 22:42 KJV).

Once again, we hear about the will of God. Think of it with an illustration. Most people, before they die, prepare a will that distributes all their worldly goods to their heirs. When death comes, the will is opened, and the executor makes sure the provisions of the will are carried out.

At the cross, God wrote his will, and sealed it with the blood of his own Son. "It is finished," Jesus cried. Nothing will erase it! There at the cross it became clear what God intended us to inherit—the forgiveness of sins and everlasting life.

He has named us his beneficiaries! So it is that when we pray "Your will be done," we no longer pray with gloomy resignation, but with a joyful eagerness. We stand to inherit all his riches. But it's even better than that. We are not only the beneficiaries of God's good will; we are also to be the executors who get to distribute his wealth to others.

Years ago I was teaching a high school Bible class. I asked the students to share their wishes. One teenaged boy replied, "I've often wished I had a million dollars." I was disappointed to hear him say that, because I had thought him a very spiritual young man who loved people more than things. "What makes you say that?" I asked with a frown. "Because," he replied with an eager look on his face, "if I had that much money, I could help a lot of people!" That answer surprised and humbled me. He was thinking about money no longer as a taker but as a giver.

Isn't that the right way to come at this prayer? We pray it as if we were the executors of God's vast estate, called to give away not money, but something better, the forgiveness and love of God. There is nothing on earth that people need more.

We have learned from Jesus to pray this prayer in a new way, with a new spirit. Lord, may your will be done by us willingly, eagerly, here on earth. Use us to bring people what you most want them to have. Teach us, Lord, to let nothing stand in our way. If you must use heartache and suffering to empty us out and make us ready vessels, do it. Give us a passion for this one thing, to bring your mercy to a crying world.

"On earth" we pray, "as it is in heaven." Dante Alighieri attempted to describe how it is in heaven. In his book *The Divine Comedy* he describes an encounter between himself and a single soul posted far out on the border of Paradise. The poet asks if she ever wishes to be closer in: "Are you desirous of a higher place, to see more?" She smiles at such an earthly question. Such a thing could not be, she replies, where our wills and God's will are unified. The happy result? "His will is our peace."[2]

It is that way in heaven. Can it be that way "on earth as it is in heaven"? Among us? It can, if we keep our eyes on Jesus Christ. If we focus on what he wanted, on how he prayed, and on why he died.

With him at the center of your vision, pray this prayer again this morning: "Your will be done." Then shall his will be done in us, and through us. And we will find our peace.

---

2. Dante, *Divine Comedy, Paradiso,* Canto III, lines 65–66, 85.

The Fourth Petition: "Our Daily Bread"

DURING THESE SUNDAYS WE are getting a master lesson on prayer, for Jesus Himself is teaching us. Today we hear him say, "This . . . is how you should pray: 'Our Father in heaven . . . give us today our daily bread'" (Matt 6:9, 11).

There it sits. Right in the middle of a prayer about important things like the will of God, the coming of his kingdom, the forgiveness of sins, and deliverance from temptation and evil, is a simple prayer for bread. What's so special about bread? Why bother about that? Shall we trouble God for a sandwich? Beg him for a piece of toast?

Actually, yes. Jesus here teaches us not to be embarrassed about that. He knows what it means to be human. He knows how hard it is for us to resist evil, work for the kingdom, or forgive sins on an empty stomach. When he hung on the cross, he said what we might well say: "I'm thirsty!"

It's hard to love God or your fellow man if you haven't had breakfast, or if the furnace goes out in mid-winter, or if you're in bed sick with the flu. Jesus teaches us here that God cares about us in body as well as in soul. He teaches us to bring God *all* of our needs, not just *some*.

"Bread" means food—whatever nourishes that body of ours. But "bread" can mean more than food. It can include all those small necessities we take so much for granted. Martin Luther asked this question in the Small Catechism: "What is meant by daily bread?" He answered his own question with a list of twenty-two items. Just listen: "Daily bread includes everything that has to do with the support and needs of the body, such as food, drink, clothing, shoes, house, home, land, animals, money, goods, a devout husband or wife, devout children, devout workers, devout and faithful rulers, good government, good weather, peace, health, self-control, good friends, faithful neighbors, and the like."[1]

1. Luther, *Small Catechism*, 20–21.

Now just imagine what it would be like if Jesus had told us not to "bother" God with all these ordinary concerns, if he had said that when we came to God in prayer, we could only speak of matters high and spiritual? Would it not leave the greater portion of our lives fatherless?

Thank God it isn't so! We have a Father all the time, who cares about all our needs, even the need for daily bread.

But why do we even need to ask? Surely the bread will come anyway, won't it? Unbelievers and atheists who never pray get their bread. But they eat. Pigs in a barnyard get fed without even knowing how to pray! Won't the bread come anyway, without our prayers?

Yes, it will. Jesus once said that God "causes his sun rise on the evil and on the good, and sends rain on the righteous and on the unrighteous" (Matt 5:45). The purpose of this prayer is not so much to make the bread come, as it is to make us receive our bread with thankful hearts. The catechism underlines it this way: "God certainly gives daily bread to everyone without our prayers, even to all evil people, but we pray in this petition that God would lead us to realize this and to receive our daily bread with thanksgiving."[2] The difference between a man and a pig is not that one eats and the other doesn't, but that one of them knows how to say "Thank you" to God.

We know how. But do we? Jesus once cured ten men of the dread disease leprosy. Only one took the trouble to thank him.

Behind all the things we receive, there is a giver, who wants to give us not merely bread, but himself as well. We have a God who constantly dignifies the little things in life by adding himself to them. Isn't that how ordinary water from a faucet becomes the sacrament of Holy Baptism? Isn't that how ordinary bread and wine become the Lord's Supper? And isn't that why Jesus tells us that in the plainest, simplest neighbor we meet, he himself comes to us?

All right. We are to ask for our bread, and all those other things we need to live. How much should we ask for? The prayer itself supplies the answer: "Give us this day our daily bread." That word "daily" comes from the Greek word *epiousion*. This word means "enough for today" or "enough for tomorrow" or possibly "enough to exist on." Whichever meaning you choose, the impact is clear. We are to ask for a minimum amount, a day's ration, just enough to keep us alive.

---

2. Luther, *Small Catechism*, 20.

The Fourth Petition: "Our Daily Bread"

What our Lord is trying to teach us, if we are willing to hear it, is that we are to be content with the necessities. That's a problem for us, because we have gotten to the point of regarding everything as a necessity, with the result that we are almost never satisfied with what we have. I heard about a man who filed for bankruptcy. The adjustor who handled the case insisted that he sell his big-screen television to help pay off his creditors. The man refused, insisting that his television was not a luxury, but a necessity. The court ruled in the man's favor!

The Bible urges us, "If we have food and clothing, we will be content with that" (1 Tim 6:8), and this prayer underlines it: "Give us this day our daily bread." But "daily" here means something more. It tells us not only *how much* we are to ask for, but also *how often* we are to pray. If I ask God today for a one-day ration of bread, it means I must ask him again tomorrow and the next day. In that way I stay close to my Heavenly Father instead of forgetting him as the days pass.

Finally, we dare not forget the smallest word in this petition - the word "us." That word is a reminder, first of all, that it is not wrong to pray for ourselves. Some of us, who were warned a lot against "selfishness" when we were young, might find this surprising. But there is no mistake. Here Jesus teaches us that God not only allows us to bring him our personal needs. He commands it.

But notice something more. The word is plural. "Give us our daily bread," not "Give me." We pray this petition not only for ourselves, but for our community, and for our world. If we are not sharing our bread, we have no right to pray this prayer! If we pray "Give us bread," doesn't that make us responsible to see to it that our own eating does not keep others from getting enough?

During the Civil War, there was a notorious prison camp called Andersonville that housed thousands of prisoners. Each day food was brought to the prison gates and left there. Although there was enough food for all the prisoners, no attempt was made at an equitable distribution. So each day prisoners made a mad rush to get their own first, and naturally the stronger and more selfish took more than they needed and hoarded it, while the weak and the sick got little or nothing. Morning after morning, guards carried out the bodies of those who had died during the night of starvation or sickness, and the next day the scene was repeated. The problem wasn't lack of food, but the unwillingness of the prisoners to share it.

If that example seems too bizarre, too remote, let me bring it closer to home. If you are an average American, you eat four and one-half pounds of food every day. For the rest of the world, the average is one and one-half. Do we stop to realize that when we pray "Give us this day our daily bread," we are praying for those hungry neighbors as well as ourselves?

Does it matter? It should matter to us. For hidden in the hungry neighbor is not just another mouth, but the Lord Jesus himself. He comes in the person of that poor, hungry one and awaits our help. "I was hungry and you fed me." That is what we will hear on Judgment Day: "Whatever you did for one of the least of these brothers of mine, you did for me" (Matt 25:40).

The joyful news I share with you, friend, is that the same Christ who comes to us in our hungry neighbor is the Christ who says, "I am the bread that came down from heaven" (John 6:41). What he commands us to give to the neighbor, he has already given to us. He gives daily bread—enough and to spare. Even more, he gives us the bread of life—his body on the cross and in the Holy Meal, full of vitamins C, B, and E (cleansing, blessed assurance, and eternal life).

When we pray this petition, let us pray it thankfully, for God is a generous giver. Let us pray it daily, lest we forget that we depend on him. And let us pray it lovingly, for we live in a hungry world.

The Fifth Petition: "Forgive Us, as We Forgive"

OUR LORD JESUS IS teaching us to pray. Today we hear him say to us: "This ... is how you should pray ... Forgive us our debts, as we also have forgiven our debtors" (Matt 6:9, 12).

It was at the post office one day that I saw a car with this bumper sticker: Christians aren't perfect—just forgiven." Indeed. We Christians are forgiven people. But that's not the whole story. Christians are also forgiving people. So close are these two things, says Jesus, that they should not (and cannot) be separated.

This morning, I want to speak to you about each one, with the goal that we might be both forgiven and forgiving.

Let's take a look at each part. First, "Forgive us our debts." Admitting our sins to God in a very general sort of way is easy to do. But to confess a specific act of wrongdoing in the presence of another human being is difficult in the extreme.

It's easy to say, "I'm a sinner," but very hard to say, "I lied to you yesterday," "I stole something from the office," "I am an alcoholic." Little children learn very early how to evade confessing a wrong. "I didn't do anything!" Or if caught red-handed, "Yeah, but he did it first!" We adults keep on doing what we learned as kids. A judge in the Midwest observed that no one ever came into his courtroom and simply confessed guilt. Everyone had some kind of excuse.

That's true because every one of us sitting here in church today has an ego, a proud self that stands like a great steel I-beam welded into our hearts. Its aim is survival, and therefore it has a terrible time admitting wrongdoing.

So it is that Jesus must teach us to say and mean the words "Father, forgive us." For in saying those words, we make a huge admission that we have rebelled and gone to war with God.

We see that warfare everywhere. In our cities there is bullying, stealing, and road rage that erupts into physical violence. In our homes husbands and wives launch verbal blasts at each other, while children smart-mouth their parents and call each other ugly names. In our churches we see warfare that often begins with the tiniest of hurts, and escalates over years into a virtual cold war of silence or gossip. People quit and whole congregations split!

In teaching us to pray this prayer, Jesus is teaching us that we are rebels who need to surrender our sin and pride and come back to God. It isn't just murderers and bank robbers. All of us need to admit it. "If we claim to be without sin, we deceive ourselves and the truth is not in us" (1 John 1:8).

There are moments when the terrible truth of our sinfulness crushes us, and we cry in desperation: "Can God forgive this? Can he forgive me?" I heard a story at a pastoral conference years ago about a Lutheran pastor in Wisconsin who received a desperate phone call on New Year's morning. On the other end of the line was a young man who had intentionally swallowed a lethal dose of drugs. "He wouldn't tell me why he was depressed," the pastor reported. "He just kept asking, 'Will God forgive me?'"

What is forgiveness? Is it simply a cover-up, as if God were like a doctor who couldn't bear to face the patient with the bad news, and so chose to ignore the x-rays and say "You're fine"? Is it simply soft-heartedness, as if God were like a judge who felt sorry for a criminal and said, "I know you're sorry, so let's just forget this indictment. Go and try a little harder to be good"?

No. Like cancer and crime, sin is a reality that must be dealt with. It is a debt to God that must be paid. The forgiveness the Bible tells us about is that God himself did the paying. Our mountainous debt has been removed, all as a gift.

Forgiveness is a gift. That means it is free, but not cheap! The cost to God was steep. He gave his only-begotten Son, and that Son paid with his blood.

But if it is already paid for, why must we ask for it? Ah, friend, the asking does not create forgiveness; the asking receives it. Let me illustrate with a small sponge and a bucket of water. I take this sponge in my hand and squeeze it tightly. Now I plunge it into a bucket of water. The water is there, all around it, but the sponge is dry (show sponge). But if I let go, the sponge is wet (show sponge). Jesus is here calling us to let go. Why hang on to our sin by denying it, by stubbornly refusing to part with it, or imagining

The Fifth Petition: "Forgive Us, as We Forgive"

foolishly that we can pay for it ourselves? Saying "Forgive us our debts" and meaning it lets go of the sin. We tell God the truth about it, part with it, and trust him to pay our debt. Are we willing to let go?

If we are willing to say, "Forgive us our debts," he will not let us stop there. We must go on to say "as we forgive our debtors." But what does "Forgive us as we forgive" mean? It all hinges on that little word "as." Is God waiting for us to go first? Surely not! Jesus tells the story of a king who forgave his servant a great debt and expected the servant to forgive his fellow in like measure. God is the one who starts this chain reaction of forgiveness.

Or are we asking God to forgive us "to the same extent" that we forgive others? Our forgiveness of others is often so grudgingly given, we'd be in trouble if this were the meaning. But neither of these is the intended sense. The Greek words, I discovered, mean "Forgive us our debts as we now, in this same moment, declare forgiveness for all who are indebted to us."

In this prayer, we are declaring total amnesty for others at the very moment we pray. Do we realize what that means? Remember the picture of the sponge? Actually, says Jesus, there are two sponges. One is my own sin. The other is the sin of my neighbor. I hold them both in the same hand. I cannot let go of one, without letting go of both. Neither can I hold on to one, without holding on to both! We cannot separate the two. If we are forgiven, we will surely forgive. If we refuse to forgive, we remain unforgiven.

All of us know this, but we try to squirm out of it somehow. Surely, we say, there must be some limit to all this forgiving. Peter asked Jesus one day, "Lord, how many times shall I forgive my brother . . . up to seven times?" Peter thought this a generous amount. Jesus answered, "I tell you, not seven times, but seventy times seven" (Matt 18:21–22). Which is to say there is no limit at all.

How hard that is for us to accept. Two young brothers were walking home from Sunday school one day, discussing how to apply this teaching to their older brother, who frequently bullied them. "I know," said the one, "we'll keep a list of how many times we forgive him." "Yeah," said the older one, "and when he gets to 491, he better watch out!"

"Where's the limit?" we ask. Do I have to forgive an abusive husband, an alcoholic wife, a rebellious teenager, a pastor who neglects me, a fellow church member who insults me? Where's the line?

Take a moment. Try to remember the worst thing someone has ever done to you. Now listen to this true story. One summer evening in 1970, a school teacher named Donald Ehrlichmann and his son Michael picked up three teenaged hitchhikers in North Minneapolis. Twenty minutes later, Ehrlichmann was dead, shot by one of the hitchhikers who had pulled a gun and demanded their wallets.

At the funeral, nearly 1000 mourners were lifted by Michael's eulogy of his father and by the amazing repose of his wife Mary. Her response to the murder was to write an open letter to the boys who had killed her husband. She said, in part, "In the quiet moments, my thoughts keep turning to you three ... I wonder to whom you are turning for comfort ... I can only pray that you come to know the love of God that fills the heart and leaves no room for hate ... If hate made you pull that trigger, I can only pray that you come to know the love of God that fills the heart and leaves no room for hate ... Know that God forgives you and that my family and I forgive you ... God keep you and bless you."[1] Do you see? There is no limit. We are called to forgive *everyone everything*.

How could Mrs. Ehrlichmann do that? How can we? We cannot, unless we look to Jesus Christ. Martin Lloyd-Jones wrote: "Whenever I see myself before God and realize something of what my Lord did for me at Calvary, I am ready to forgive anybody anything. I cannot withhold it. I no longer even want to withhold it."[2] We remember how he said, even as they crucified him, "Father, forgive them" (Luke 23:34). We cannot turn others away without turning him away as well.

Brothers and sisters, there is an urgency in this. So many of us hold inside some old resentment we cannot let go. Until we do, says our Lord, we stand in danger of losing our very souls.

Is there some person you are angry with? Resolve that you will call, or write, or even visit that person this week and say with God's help: "I have stored this resentment for so long, I can do it no longer. Because of Jesus, I forgive you, and I pray that if I have hurt you, you will forgive me."

Before us is the cross. Was it in vain he died there? Or will we find the purpose as we pray, "Forgive us, as we forgive"?

God grant that what we pray we may put into practice.

---

1. Klobuchar, *You Killed My Husband,* pars 7–18.
2. Lloyd-Jones, *Christian Quotes,* par 1.

The Sixth Petition: "Lead Us not into Temptation"

SOMEWHERE IN EASTERN GERMANY stands to this day an ancient castle called The Wartburg. There more than 500 years ago, Martin Luther lived for many months in disguise, hiding from his enemies and translating the Bible into German. Centuries later, visitors touring that castle could see a large ink stain on the wall of Luther's old study. Guides told them the story of how Luther once felt so sorely tempted by the Devil that he turned and flung an inkwell at him, smashing it against the wall.

Modern people are inclined to chuckle at such a story. Many don't take the Devil seriously and therefore don't consider temptation such a serious matter either.

What about you? Do you ever wrestle with temptation? Have you ever felt like throwing something at the Devil? Or do we, like so many moderns, think all of this is just a lot of old-fashioned talk?

Ponder the fact that Jesus himself warns insistently about the danger of temptation. As we continue our series on the Lord's Prayer, we hear him say, "This . . . is how you should pray ... lead us not into temptation" (Matt 6:9, 13).

What is temptation? The word Jesus uses in this prayer literally means "testing" or "trial." What is on trial is our relationship with God, our willingness to believe his Word and obey him.

We have spoken of the Devil as an agent of temptation. The two best-known Bible stories about temptation portray him as the tempter. In one, the serpent in the Garden of Eden tempts Eve. In the other, Satan confronts Jesus in the wilderness. In both he uses same strategy. Like a fisherman, he baits his hook and hides it beneath pious-sounding words: "You will be like God, knowing good and evil" (Gen 3:5). "He will command his angels concerning you" (Matt 4:6). But underneath the words is a sharp hook—the same hook he would use to snare you and pull you away from simple obedience to God.

But there are other enemies, other agents of temptation. In the Small Catechism, Luther mentions that "the devil, the world, and our sinful nature may . . . deceive us or mislead us into false belief, despair, and other great shame and vice."[1]

What form does temptation take? Too often, when we hear this word temptation, we think immediately of some obvious, spectacular wickedness. A pastor friend of mine reported what happened to him when he was attending a pastoral conference at a hotel in Detroit. The evening meeting had ended, and this man was headed back to his room. In the dark, deserted hallway, he was accosted by a strange woman who propositioned him. "Now that's a temptation!" we say. No mistaking that variety.

But it does not usually come to us in such an obvious way. It may come quietly, on the lips of your boss, or your spouse. It may be something as simple as the invitation to tell a small lie, cheat on a time sheet, skip church "just this once," or to listen and laugh at some slander about a person you both despise. Learn this prayer well, for we can be certain that temptation will come to each of us. Whether sudden or gradual, a large sin or a small one, the Tempter's goal is always the same. He aims to separate us from God. In his popular book *The Screwtape Letters*, C. S. Lewis has a senior devil give the following advice to an apprentice tempter: "You will say that these are very small sins; and, doubtless, like all young tempters, you are anxious to be able to report spectacular wickedness. But do remember, the only thing that matters is the extent to which you separate the man from the Enemy."[2]

It can happen anywhere. On the job may come the temptation to use foul language, despise the boss, or let the job itself come between you and worship. At home watching television is a prime time to promote the wasting of time, the neglect of prayer, and the cultivation of coveting the goods dangled before us at commercial breaks. Nor are we safe at church. Right here there are temptations aplenty to gossip, to complain, or to feel self-righteous.

Indeed, in the hands of the Devil, almost anything can become a temptation. So Jesus warns us to pray, "Lead us not into temptation." The

---

1. Luther, *Small Catechism*, 21.
2. Lewis, *Screwtape Letters*, 56.

The Sixth Petition: "Lead Us not into Temptation"

words are more than a warning. They contain the implicit promise that we are coming to a God who both hears and helps as we face the temptation.

That help comes in several ways. First, he shields us from some temptations so that we never meet them at all. Isn't that why we say, "Lead us not into . . ."? We might say it in a different way. "Keep us clear of temptation" or perhaps "Help us avoid facing temptation."

When God does this, of course, we will not be aware of it, any more than we are aware of an accident that didn't happen as we came to church this morning.

Speaking of coming to church, did any of you pray before you came to church that you would be protected from saying something sinful here this morning? Sad to say, we rarely pray the prayer this way. We rarely pray about temptation at all until we find ourselves surrounded by it. We are like those sleepy disciples in Gethsemane. Our Lord warned them and warns us: "Watch and pray so that you will not fall into temptation" (Mark 14:38), but we don't sense the nearness of the danger until one day when we wake up and find that some powerful temptation has us by the throat!

That brings us to a second kind of help God gives—the provision of an escape hatch. Paul says in 1 Corinthians 10:13, "God is faithful, and he will not let you be tempted beyond what you can bear. But when you are tempted, he will also provide a way out."

This is especially important with temptations that are more or less unavoidable, the kind we know we will be facing tomorrow. You may be a student at school who knows that tomorrow, as always, you will be teased, or bullied, or invited to bad-mouth your teacher. You may be dating someone and know that this week, as always, you will face sexual temptation. You may be a worker who knows that tomorrow, as always, you will face the sniping comments of a fellow worker who makes your blood boil.

How important that we pray before we get into such situations, not only for strength, but for a way of escape, if necessary. Luther said memorably: "**you cannot prevent the birds from flying over your head but you can keep them from building a nest in your hair**"[3]

But it is just there, isn't it, that we face our worst problem? For isn't there inside each one of us a part that welcomes temptation with open arms, that practically begs those birds to build their nests? God himself tempts no one, writes James, "but each one is tempted when, by his own evil desire, he is dragged away and enticed" (Jas 1:14).

---

3. Warren, *Purpose-Driven Life,* 205

And what help is there for us who have already yielded, those in whose hair the birds have already built their nests, in whom the Devil has already set his deadly hook? Friend, remember who it is that teaches us this prayer. Jesus himself kneels down beside us. He who teaches us to pray about temptation joins in the fight against it.

First he forgives our failures. In a moment of weakness, Peter had yielded to fear's temptation and denied his Lord. How crushed he was. How bitterly he wept! Yet there was the risen Lord with a hand on Peter's shoulder, with a call, "Feed my sheep," (John 21:17) and the implicit assurance, "All is forgiven." If you have fallen, don't be afraid. Ask his pardon. Take his hand.

But go further. Now that you know your weakness, ask that he stand beside you from now on, and put up a resistance. For he knows your enemy the Devil. He faced him down in the Wilderness and conquered him with a word. He faced him on the cross and conquered him with his blood. His power is now yours, as you ask it in this petition and in the one to follow: "Deliver us from evil."

One night a young policeman on patrol duty spotted something moving inside a dimly-lit store as he drove past. Sensing trouble, he stopped his car and radioed for backup. Then he entered the store. Once inside, he found two thieves at work. In the ensuing scuffle, the patrolman was thrown to the floor unconscious. But as one of his assailants drew a knife, a backup officer burst through the door with gun drawn. The young officer was spared.

Such help Christ Jesus offers us! He knows our danger, and so he instructs us to call on him as our backup, perhaps in the person of another Christian who can serve as a prayer partner.

Having done that, we need fear nothing, for there is nothing we face alone. Call on Him. Then fight the good fight.

If necessary, launch an inkwell.

The Seventh Petition: "Deliver Us from Evil"

During these weeks, we have come to our Lord, asking Him: "Lord, teach us to pray." Today we hear him say, "This . . . is how you should pray . . . deliver us from evil" (Matt 6:9, 13).

This petition may be the last, but it is surely not the least. It is no afterthought, not a P.S. tacked on to the end of the prayer. Our need for deliverance from evil is as constant as our need for daily bread and as urgent as the coming of God's kingdom.

For evil meets us everywhere. There are no "safe" places in the world. At a nursing home in Missouri, residents were repeatedly robbed and assaulted by staff members until newly-installed surveillance cameras caught them in the act. At a daycare center in Washington State, parents were dumbfounded to learn that some of the children had been molested by workers there. Stay at any hotel in the prettiest, most peaceful spot you can find, and you will see locks on all the doors and the warning posted prominently: "Not responsible for stolen items." It's that kind of world.

Jesus knows this world well, so he teaches us to pray, "Deliver us from evil." There is more to this simple prayer than meets the eye. In the original Greek text is a little word that most Bible translations leave out, the definite article "the." Translated literally, this petition reads "Deliver us from *the* evil," which is to say, "from the evil one," the Devil. That little word is a reminder that when we pray this prayer, we are asking for help, not merely with an assortment of problems that happen *to* us, like auto accidents, disease, and crime, but with a sinister evil that lies *within* us and a fearsome enemy who wages war *against* us.

People don't want to believe that. There is a tendency these days to minimize evil and hope thereby to explain it away. Years ago, for example, alcoholism began to be described as "a sickness, not a sin." But sickness and sin are not so easily separated. Certain mental disorders and socially-destructive behaviors are traced to chemical imbalances or genetic anomalies, but scientists admit that such explanations are only pieces of a larger puzzle of human behavior.

Many of our best efforts to change human behavior seem to make hardly a dent, and billions of dollars spent on education, drug therapy, and counseling bring only small returns, for evil runs deep in this world, and there is no easy deliverance.

We must pray for deliverance from evil, says our Lord, because in the end it will come in no other way, and from no one else but God. That means, very simply, we cannot deliver ourselves.

I heard a story about two young men who were "off-roading" and drove their car inadvertently into an abandoned mine shaft. The car plunged downward and became wedged in the shaft in such a way that the boys were unable to exit the car and climb to safety. Their only resource was a pack of matches. For three days they sat and burned pieces of the car, hoping against hope that a passerby might see the smoke. Finally they were down to their last match. "We prayed real hard," said one of the boys. Incredibly, someone did see the smoke, and they were rescued shortly thereafter.

Like those boys, we are trapped by evil, helpless to climb out of it by ourselves. Help, if it comes at all, must come from outside us.

Some are convinced that such help is to be found in "experts." In our society, we place tremendous burdens on teachers, politicians, counselors, and doctors, but we discover that the help they can give is limited. When an election is over, we learn all over again that our nation's problems are bigger than all the promises politicians can make, however well-intentioned. At the hospital, the doctor finally must admit, "I'm sorry—there is nothing more I can do." Teachers aren't miracle-workers, and counselors say that it all depends on whether we want to help ourselves.

Finally we are left like those two boys—wedged in by evil. There is nothing left but to "pray real hard." That turns out to be the right thing, for no human being can deliver us from evil. Only God can. Therefore we pray to him: "Father, deliver us from evil."

Deliverance is his specialty. So wrote the Psalmist: "Deliverance belongs to the Lord" (Ps 3:8 RSV). The very name "Jesus" means "Savior." And that brings us back to the one who is teaching us to pray this prayer. Each week we have seen that Jesus gives us what he teaches us to pray for. So also here. He teaches us to say, "Deliver us from evil" with confident voices, for he himself is our Deliverer.

The Seventh Petition: "Deliver Us from Evil"

How does He do it? Well, how did those two boys get rescued? Did someone call them on a cell phone to offer good advice? Did someone send them a hope-filled e-mail? No. Someone showed up on the scene in person, in the flesh.

That's the very first thing Jesus did. One of the old Christmas hymns proclaims it: "He came down to earth from heaven, who is God and Lord of all. And His shelter was a stable, and his cradle was a stall." But it wasn't the last thing He did!

In Hebrews 2:14–15 we read: "He too shared in their humanity so that by his death he might destroy him who hold the power of death—that is, the devil—and free those who all their lives were held in slavery by their fear of death." Destroy the Devil? Yes he does. Deliver us from slavery and sin? Yes he does.

But did you notice how? Through death. The surprising way that Jesus delivers us from death, devil, and all evil is by literally traveling through death and emerging on the other side.

And now for the hardest thing of all. The only way any of us may finally be delivered from evil is if we die with him. Is that crazy? Impossible? No, it isn't. As a matter of fact, our dying has already started. That's what happened back at the baptismal font. The old, evil part of us began to die.

The old Adam was shoved under the water to drown, and a great battle began. For the old Adam (or the old Eve, as the case may be), puts up a desperate fight to re-emerge and take control again. Can you feel that inner struggle? God allies himself with us in that fight, and he will do almost anything, use almost any means, to deliver us from evil.

Let me ask you a simple question: "What do you think God most wants for you?" That you live to be ninety years old in unbroken good health? That you become a millionaire? What we read instead in the Bible is that God wants us to know him, to live with a joyful faith in him. His aim is not our happiness, but our holiness.

That means he will even allow suffering or pain to enter our lives, if by it we can be separated from sin and evil, because in the end, on the other side of our physical death, he plans to give our lives back to us, clean and whole again.

Many decades ago, I watched God work in such a mysterious way in the life of a man named Larry. Larry was a man in his late thirties, married with two children. He had a steady job as a lumber salesman that paid him well. But in spite of his outward success, Larry's life was not happy. For years he had been drifting away from the Lord. His first marriage went bad and ended in divorce, and he began to drink too much. His attitude toward the church was increasingly hostile. He remarried, but that marriage too went sour. He and his second wife began arguing constantly and were separated.

One night he went to the bar where she worked and they had a terrible argument. He left in a rage and sped home in his car, but on the way he lost control and smashed into a tree. For days, Larry hovered near death in the hospital. As he regained strength, the doctor brought bitter news. Larry was paralyzed from the neck down. It was in the hospital that I met Larry, and we began a friendship that lasted a long time.

Larry was eventually able to go home, but he had to learn to live life all over again. During that time, I watched a miracle take place. Larry's bitterness at the church and his distance from God melted away. There grew again a faith in God that had nearly died with him. He came back to church and even joined a home Bible study group.

One day several years after the accident, Larry said to me, "Pastor, I want you to know that I can give thanks to God for what happened to me that night. Don't get me wrong. I wouldn't wish this on anyone else. But if God had not allowed me to get in that accident, I think my life would have gone down the drain. I'd be dead by now, and I would be in hell. But I know that one day, I'll be in heaven with God, and I'll have a new body."

That is what this prayer is all about. We have a God who delivers, not merely from physical sickness and financial debts and broken relationships but from the greater evil that lies beneath. He delivers, not always in the way we expect, but often through the very heartaches and losses that life brings.

Deliver us from evil. It is also a prayer for the present moment, that none of the "evils" we face today will pull us from our Father's arms. It is also a prayer for the future, that God might "graciously take us from this valley of sorrow to Himself in heaven,"[1] as the catechism puts it so beautifully.

Come to him with your helplessness and bondage. Give him your weakness and fear. See before you the Savior Jesus Christ. Pray with solid trust, and he will deliver you.

He can, you know, for his is the kingdom, and the power, and the glory, forever and ever. Amen.

---

1. Luther, *Small Catechism*, 22.

The Sacrament of Holy Baptism

Baptism One – "Born Again"

OUR TEXT IS JOHN 3:1–8: "Now there was a man of the Pharisees named Nicodemus, a member of the Jewish ruling council. He came to Jesus at night and said, 'Rabbi, we know that you are a teacher who has come from God. For no one could perform the signs you are doing if God were not with him.' In reply Jesus declared, 'I tell you the truth, no one can see the kingdom of God unless he is born again.' 'How can a man be born when he is old?' Nicodemus asked. 'Surely he cannot enter a second time into his mother's womb to be born!' Jesus answered, 'I tell you the truth, no one can enter the kingdom of God unless he is born of water and the Spirit. Flesh gives birth to flesh, but the Spirit gives birth to spirit. You should not be surprised at my saying, "You must be born again." The wind blows wherever it pleases. You hear its sound, but you cannot tell where it comes from or where it is going. So it is with everyone born of the Spirit.'"

In the city of Reno, Nevada, is a contemporary picture of an ancient truth. It's Bill Harrah's auto collection, now housed in the National Automobile Museum. On display are 200 cars, domestic and foreign, each restored to gleaming perfection. One appreciates the accomplishment all the more when one sees the rusting frames and battered carcasses of autos awaiting restoration in the junkyard nearby.

How much time, skill, and money it takes to restore just one junked car! How much *more* it takes to restore a human being whose life has been battered and scarred by sin.

Not just a little repair work, but a total restoration is needed. Jesus said it this way: "You must be born again" (John 3:7). Those were his words to a man named Nicodemus. Nicodemus was no derelict, no commoner. He was intelligent and respected—a ruler of the Jews who sat on the highest governing body in the land.

But Nicodemus was troubled. That night as he stepped out of the shadows into the moonlight to meet Jesus, his heart must have been anxious. On the outside, he appeared dignified and in control, but on the inside he was restless, searching. He knew something in his life needed to change, but he didn't know what. So he came seeking this man, of whom he had heard so much. "I must meet him tonight," Nicodemus had told himself.

What Nicodemus heard that night was more than he had bargained for. He had expected a theological discussion. To be sure, he had expected to learn something from this young rabbi. But he was not prepared for what he heard: "You must be born again."

People today are still astounded by the idea. Yes, Jesus was a fine man. Yes, a good teacher. He'll teach us right from wrong, give us steps to take toward moral improvement, show us how to be more religious, surely. That's what we expect. Instead we hear this strange sermon: "You must be born again."

Christianity still proclaims what Jesus told Nicodemus that night. God does not want "nicer" people—He wants completely new creatures. Not a "makeover," but a new birth. No one will enter the kingdom of God without it, because, explains Jesus, "Flesh gives birth to flesh" (John 3:6). To rephrase it, sinful parents don't produce sinless children.

We make light of it. "Nobody's perfect," we say, reducing sin to a modest and altogether manageable imperfection—something like crooked teeth that can be pulled into line by wearing braces for a while.

If that's our view of sin, religion becomes nothing more than a repair job, a series of personality adjustments, a matter of trying harder and harder to "be good." In the same way, I suppose, one might teach a horse to jump higher and further. But the gap between us and God is simply too enormous, says Paul: "Flesh and blood cannot inherit the kingdom of God" (1 Cor 15:50). It's as if we had brought our poor horse to the edge of the Grand Canyon and urged it to jump across. No horse, no matter how well-bred or well-trained, could manage such a leap. Only if that horse became a different creature, only if it grew wings like Pegasus, could it hope to cover that distance.

We are only flesh and blood, said Jesus. If we are to come back to God, it can only happen by becoming new creatures. "You must be born again." "But how?" retorted Nicodemus. "You're talking nonsense. You're asking the impossible!" We say the same. "I'm the way I am. I'll never change. God is asking too much."

Baptism One – "Born Again"

Look again at that phrase Jesus uses. "Born again" has a double meaning in Greek. We can translate it as we did: "Born again." Born a second time. But the same words can also be translated "Born from above." From above. That is to say, this is something God must do in us. We cannot do this by ourselves any more than a baby can conceive itself or give itself birth.

There's an old fable about a farmer who decided to transplant a brier bush into his rose garden. The bush protested, "I'll never produce anything but thorns!" Nevertheless, the farmer went ahead. After transplanting that bush, he grafted a rose stalk onto the top of the brier. When summer came, the brier was astonished at the beautiful pink roses it bore. "How did I do that?" asked the brier. "Your beauty," replied the farmer, "is not something you produced, but something I have given you."

Born again means "Born from above." God reaches down and grafts us into Jesus Christ. There's no other way to become new creatures, except by letting God attach us to Jesus Christ. Nicodemus found it mystifying: "How can this be?" In answer, Jesus' strange sermon gets even stranger. "Of water and the spirit," Jesus explains (John 3:5).

The new birth comes in Holy Baptism. There we are grafted into Christ. There the old self dies and a new self is born. God has given us no other way to be born again. That's what Peter preached to the throng at Pentecost: "Repent and be baptized, every one of you" (Acts 2:38).

If you spend much time in a Lutheran Church, this is probably not news to you. We have our baptisms, most often, right in front of the congregation on a Sunday morning. We sing hymns about baptism. Recite the catechism sections on it too.

The grace and saving power of Holy Baptism is a message that needs increasingly to be heard in our country these days. People talk of being "born again," but there is rarely mention of baptism in that discussion. Billy Graham was one of the most powerful evangelists in the last generation, worthy of great admiration. But in one particular, his message was puzzling. Graham wrote an entire book on this subject entitled *How to be Born Again*. Though excellent in many ways, it has a surprising omission. Nowhere in the book does he say anything about being baptized!

What we hear from many fellow Christians is talk of making a decision for Christ, or of having a personal experience of being saved. The result is that many people who do believe in Jesus and have been baptized come to doubt their salvation. They wonder if, perhaps, they are not really true Christians. They wonder if they ought to make some new decision or have a different set of experiences.

There is nothing wrong with having memorable experiences, feeling soaring emotions, or making commitments to obey the Lord, so long as we remember that God is the subject, the "doer" in all this, that the new birth is his doing and that it is sealed in Holy Baptism.

For commitments waver. Emotions are unpredictable. Experiences may deceive. But nothing can undo the action of God. It stands certain and sure: I have been baptized. There God gave me a new birth.

Does it seem astounding to claim so much for such a simple act? We hear the splash of water and a few spoken words. How can it be that a whole new life is born here? It is like the wind, Jesus told Nicodemus. You can hear the sound it makes and watch the tree branches swaying at its touch. But you will never fully understand where it comes from, or where it goes. It remains mysterious.

The mysterious power of Baptism is rooted in the Word of God. "How can water do such great things?" Luther asks in the Small Catechism. It is "certainly not just water," he explains, "but the word of God in and with the water does these things, along with the faith which trusts this word of God in the water."[1] God commands us to receive it in faith and hold fast to his promise that here a new life begins.

Begins, yes. But the new life *begun* must also be *lived*. That is the message we need to hear from those in the Born Again Movement. For there are people who have been born again, who have been baptized, who bear no fruit. They have stopped growing, stopped living a redeemed life. Their love for the Lord has grown cold.

So it is that those who are born again must be "reborn" daily and renewed in that long-ago baptism, in the way couples married long ago must find daily renewal in their marriages.

Years ago, Dr. Martin Marty, a Lutheran professor at the University of Chicago, was being interviewed on a TV talk show by a Baptist host. The conversation turned to the "Born Again Movement." The interviewer teasingly asked if Marty was born again. Without hesitation Marty replied that he was born again in 1928, when he was baptized, and that he was born again every day afterward.

So it is with the life God gives. Daily it is to be reclaimed, renewed, and lived out in repentance and faith, or it may die. "What does such baptizing

---

1. Luther, *Small Catechism*, 24

Baptism One – "Born Again"

with water indicate?" Luther went on to ask in the Small Catechism. "It indicates that the old Adam in us should by daily contrition and repentance be drowned and die with all sins and evil desires, and that a new man should daily emerge and arise to live before God in righteousness and purity forever."[2] Day after day!

What Marty was asked, I will ask you. Have you been born again? If not, hear this sermon as God's invitation to you. If you, like most others here today, have been born again, make the most of it. Rejoice in it. Reclaim it day after day.

Like a married couple that stands to renew their vows, stand again before the Lord today. Confess the sin. Trust his promised pardon. Claim his Holy Spirit's power for daily, fruitful living. Let him strengthen what began so long ago in your baptism.

---

2. Luther, *Small Catechism*, 25.

Baptism Two - "Christ's Baptism and Mine"

OUR TEXT IS LUKE 3:21–22. "When all the people were being baptized, Jesus was baptized too. And as he was praying, heaven was opened and the Holy Spirit descended on him in bodily form, like a dove. And a voice came from heaven: 'You are my Son, whom I love; with you I am well pleased.'"

It can properly be said that everything Jesus did was done for us. We sing it at Christmas: "Jesus was born for us." We say it on Good Friday: "Jesus died for us." We shout it on Easter: "Jesus rose for us!"

But when it comes to his baptism, we fall curiously silent. I have rarely heard anyone say, "Jesus was baptized for me." Indeed, of all the things Jesus did, this act was one of the most puzzling. It must be important, for all four of the Gospels report it, a fact not the case with his birth, his sermon on the mount, or his institution of the Lord's Supper. Yet, for most of us, the purpose of that baptism remains hazy.

Yes, he was baptized. But why? What good did it do for the sinless Son of God to submit to this sinner's bath? And what good did it do for me, who had to have my own baptism so many years ago? Let's look again at this brief story from the life of Jesus, so that each of us might see the connection between Christ's baptism and mine.

To help us remember, I will use three words beginning with the letter "b": beginning, bestowing, and belonging.

First, Christ's baptism was a beginning. It came, not in the middle, but at the very start of his ministry. By this time Jesus is thirty years old, and his growing up years have been wrapped in obscurity. Luke gives only a brief glimpse of his boyhood in the story of twelve-year-old Jesus left behind in Jerusalem at Passover and finally found in the Temple after a three-day search by his parents.

We hunger for more details, but the Bible is ruthlessly silent. We know nothing of his teen years, nothing of his work, though it is almost certain

Baptism Two - "Christ's Baptism and Mine"

that, like other Jewish boys, he took up his father's work, carpentry. But today, here at the Jordan River, those eighteen years of silence are shattered. Jesus strides out of nowhere to be baptized by his cousin John the Baptist.

That baptism is a beginning. Like the starter's gun at a track meet, it propels Jesus into a whirlwind of activity. Disciples are gathered. Sermons are preached. The sick are healed. Demons cast out. Hungry crowds are fed in a miraculous way. From this moment on, the pace is frenetic, and it does not slacken until his enemies nail him to the cross.

His baptism was a beginning. So is yours and mine. "What shall we do?" the crowd asked Peter at Pentecost. "Repent and be baptized," he answered (Acts 2:37-38). The mass baptism of 3000 people that day launched them into the new life marked by the apostles' teaching, fellowship, the breaking of bread at the Lord's Table, and prayer. Baptism was the launching pad, the doorway into the Christian life.

In many ancient churches, the baptismal font was placed at the entrance to the church to signify that baptism was the beginning, the doorway into the Christian life. For most of us, it was literally so. It was the very first "Christian" thing done to us.

That is both a comfort and a challenge. It is a comfort when I wonder about whether or not I am a Christian. If I slip, if I fail, if I fall, I need not start all over again, for the beginning was already made. God set me on the path. I simply need to return to it and continue on my way.

But it is also a challenge. The very word "beginning" implies that something must now follow—the daily obedience of Christ and service of my neighbor. Those who bring a child to baptism but then neglect instruction, worship, and prayer are deceiving themselves and despising this sacrament. The sprinter must get out of his blocks, but he must also finish the race.

So it is that God has made this sacrament not only the beginning, but also a crucial bestowing. With the water and the Word God bestows a great gift that helps us finish our race. Jesus received it in an unforgettable way. Luke tells us, "heaven was opened and the Holy Spirit descended on him in bodily form like a dove" (Luke 3:22).

That gift was essential for Jesus' ministry. It is striking that Jesus healed no one, cast out no demons, preached no sermons until he was baptized. With the Holy Spirit came the power he needed for everything else.

Your baptism was God bestowing you with an indispensable survival kit. Luther asks in his catechism: "What benefits does baptism give?" Then he answers his own question: "It works forgiveness of sins, rescues from death and the devil, and gives eternal salvation to all who believe this, as the words and promises of God declare."[1]

He says it, not on his own authority, but on that of Saint Paul, who wrote to Titus: "He saved us through the washing of rebirth and renewal by the Holy Spirit . . . so that, having been justified by his grace, we might become heirs having the hope of eternal life" (Titus 3:5–7).

All of that happened to you and to me when we were baptized. No, the rafters did not shake. Nor have I heard reports that any doves were seen fluttering down over the font. But God's promise is sure: "For we were all baptized by one Spirit . . . and we were all given the one Spirit to drink" (1 Cor 12:13). That's the same Holy Spirit that empowered Jesus for his ministry.

Why is it, then, that we so often feel powerless? Why do so many Christians, though baptized, later run off in search of something to revive their sagging spirits? Why do some even seek a second baptism "in the Holy Spirit"? Did the first one fail?

Indeed not. It is we who have failed to use the gift God graciously bestowed. If I've been given a new coat, it won't do to leave it hanging in the closet each morning. I must put it on.

God gave us his Holy Spirit long ago. Do we leave the Spirit hanging in the closet, or do we daily "put him on" with prayer so that we may be clothed with his power? Do we daily pick up the "sword of the Spirit," the Word of God that is the essential weapon of our daily warfare?

Baptism is a bestowing of the Holy Spirit. "Since we live by the Spirit," urges Paul, "let us keep I step with the Spirit" (Gal 5:25). In other words, *use* the Spirit God gave you by reading his Word and praying for his presence and power.

But there was even more in Christ's baptism, and more in ours. That day Jesus heard his Father speak these words, "You are my Son, whom I love; with you I am well pleased" (Luke 3:22). When you were baptized, God said it to you unmistakably: "You are my own dear child. You belong to me!"

Baptism is, most beautifully, a sacrament of belonging. How desperately we need to hear that, know that. The toddler huddled in his mother's lap, the teenaged lovers walking arm-in-arm down school hallways, and the

---

1. Luther, *Small Catechism*, 24.

Baptism Two - "Christ's Baptism and Mine"

old folks in their apartments waiting for the phone to ring are all hungry to belong to someone.

The beauty of baptism is that here God says unmistakably, "You do! You are mine." So it was for a man named Jerry. Abandoned as a child, Jerry grew up in an orphanage, one of those unfortunate children who never knew his parents. But Jerry had someone to hang onto. There was a man who visited that orphanage. One day he asked the staff if he might take Jerry to church and have him baptized. The day came and the deed was done. Though Jerry was too young to remember it, that man never let him forget that he was baptized. He had a heavenly Father. He belonged to someone who loved him. Years later, nurtured by that love, Jerry became a Lutheran pastor in Oregon. His special gift was his ability to show care to the teenagers who flocked to his youth group. "You are baptized," he told them. "You belong to God!"

And just here we see how Christ's baptism and our own come together. Now we understand why Jesus submitted to the sinner's bath that day. In that act, He says, "Now I belong to you!" He came "to be sin for us, who knew no sin." He submits to the washing we need. He died the death we deserved. He joins hands with us, takes our sins upon himself, makes our griefs and burdens his own. The righteous robe he wore, he places on us.

His baptism was the beginning of his ministry of love. It continues each time a child or an adult is brought to this font. Remember it. Give thanks for it. And take heart in it.

We are baptized. We are his. And he is ours.

Office of the Keys (Confession)

Office of the Keys One - "I Give You the Keys"

OUR TEXT IS MATTHEW 16:16–19. "Simon Peter answered, 'You are the Messiah, the Son of the living God.' Jesus replied, 'Blessed are you, Simon son of Jonah, for this was not revealed to you by flesh and blood, but by my Father in heaven. And I tell you that you are Peter, and on this rock I will build my church, and the gates of Hades will not overcome it. I will give you the keys of the kingdom of heaven; whatever you bind on earth will be bound in heaven, and whatever you loose on earth will be loosed in heaven.' Then he ordered his disciples not to tell anyone that he was the Messiah."

This word of Jesus about the giving of the keys brings to mind a dramatic scene from the movie *Titanic*. The ship has struck an iceberg and is sinking. Below decks, Jack and Rose scramble up the stairs toward a possible rescue. The water is rising fast behind them. But they find they are trapped behind a metal mesh gate. They plead with a passing crewman to open it for them. He hesitates, then turns, pulls out his keys, and fumbles with them in a panic as the water rises. Finally he drops the keys into the water and flees. The viewer wonders, "What will happen to them? Will they retrieve the keys and open the door before it is too late?"

Though it is never that dramatic, we all know the sinking feeling of being locked out. You're late for a meeting, but you can't find your car keys. Or you're locked out of your own house, seeing your purse on the table through the window. You need something from a file drawer, but can't open it. You arrive at a restaurant, pull on the front door, and see that it closed just minutes ago. In each case, you need to get in, but can't. It may produce a feeling of desperation, or simply frustration. Who has that key when we need it?

Jesus used that common experience to warn us of a much more dreadful prospect. In his parable of the foolish maidens who are unprepared and late for the wedding banquet, he sums up their fate in four words: "the door was shut" (Matt 25:10). Their pleading was to no avail. They were locked out!

That wedding feast is Jesus' picture of the eternal life and joy that awaits those who are allowed to enter the kingdom of heaven. The warning for us? It's possible to find ourselves on the outside looking in. Our stubborn sins separate us from God as surely as if a heavy door were closed and locked against us. When the Day of Judgment comes, will the door swing open as he says, "Come, you who are blessed by my Father," or will it remain shut as he says, "Depart from me" (Matt 25:34, 41)?

This text in Matthew 16 brings the great good news that there are keys fashioned to open that door and bring us to safety. Jesus himself has them. Even better is the news that he entrusts those keys to us: "I will give you the keys of the kingdom of heaven."

How can we be good stewards of those keys for ourselves and other people? Let's think further about each part of this picture.

We begin with the door. The very existence of doors and locks everywhere we go is a forceful reminder of this dangerous world and our own fallen humanity. If humans weren't prone to violence and theft, we wouldn't need to lock our doors. But in fact we do. Locks on doors keep out those who would hurt us.

The door in Matthew 16 is the door of "the kingdom of heaven." The fact that heaven has a door is a sobering reminder that salvation is not guaranteed. Some will come in and be saved. Others will be locked out and lost. Not all will even find that door, for it is narrow. When the disciples asked Jesus how many would be saved, he told them that the door was narrow and "only a few" would find it. Jesus himself is that door. "I am the door," he told the disciples (John 10:9 KJV). "No one comes to the Father except through me" (John 14:6).

Not all of those who hear about Jesus will be able to go in. Some will find the door locked against them because they persist in their sins. Paul warned the Corinthians that "neither . . . thieves nor the greedy nor drunkards nor slanderers nor swindlers will inherit the kingdom of God" (1 Cor 6:9–10). Our sins close and lock the door to eternal life. The good news of the Gospel is that there is hope for sinners, those on the outside. God has made provision for those who are locked out by their sins to find entry again.

That brings us to the second part of this picture—the keys. Keys differ widely from each other. There are flat keys, tubular keys, skeleton keys, and

Office of the Keys One - "I Give You the Keys"

more. Generally only one key will fit the lock and open it. On your personal key ring you may have half a dozen keys or more, and after long experience you know which is your car key, your house key, the keys to your office or the padlock on your tool shed.

There is one key that opens heaven's door. Only one! People try to open it with keys of their own making. At funerals, for example, people say, "She was a good person," or "He worked hard and never hurt anyone." That sounds hopeful, but those "keys" will not work. There is only one key that will work. The key God made to unlock us from our sins and open the door of heaven is cross-shaped.

Jesus fashioned that key when he went to the cross and rose from death. He is now the keeper of the keys. "I hold the keys of death and Hades," says the risen Christ in Revelation 1:18. The Gospel of Jesus is the only key that opens. That's why Paul wrote to the Corinthians, "I resolved to know nothing while I was with you except Jesus Christ and him crucified" (1 Cor 2:2). That's what Paul and Silas offered the Philippian jailer: "Believe in the Lord Jesus Christ and you will be saved" (Acts 16:31).

The astonishing thing in this text from Matthew is that Jesus entrusts his keys to us! Some of us may remember the momentous day our parents entrusted us with the keys to the family car. It was awesome to be so trusted. Now that we are adults with children of our own, we understand what a gift it was.

In Matthew's version, of course, it is Peter himself who is the recipient. But in the parallel account in John 20, the privilege is given to all the apostles.

That brings us to the third element in this picture to consider. For a key has not one function, but two—locking and unlocking. Here in the text Jesus speaks of "binding" and "loosing." If those words are puzzling, the parallel in John 20 makes things crystal clear: "If you forgive anyone ... they are forgiven; if you do not forgive them, they are not forgiven" (John 20:23).

This holy work that Jesus entrusts to us has, therefore, been called "The Office of the Keys." The Small Catechism defines it this way: "The Office of the Keys is that authority which Christ gave the church to forgive the sins of those who repent, but to declare to those who do not repent that their sins are not forgiven."[1] His authority, given to us to exercise on his behalf. "Take these keys of mine," he says, "and use them well!"

1. Luther, *Small Catechism*, 29

That, of course, is the great challenge. How do we use these keys aright? It all depends on who is doing the sinning. Who stands outside that locked door?

We must, Jesus makes clear, start with our own sin before we confront the neighbor's sin. The log in my own eye before the speck in his! When I am the sinner, I am standing outside the door, and it is locked and bolted against me. I am desperate to have the door opened again. Who will do it for me? There are three who can—the person I have sinned against, a confessor who will hear my confession, and God himself.

A basic truth in every Christian's life—in yours and mine too—is that when I am the sinner, I am to confess it and seek forgiveness. It may happen publicly in the worship service as we speak the words together: "I, a poor, miserable sinner, confess unto thee all my sins and iniquities" and then hear the pastor speak the absolution: "Upon this your confession, I as a called and ordained servant of the Word, announce the grace of God to all of you, and in the stead and by the command of my Lord Jesus Christ, I forgive you . . ." The pastor is using those keys Jesus entrusted to us all. What a joy to hear and know that Jesus loves and forgives!

Or it may happen privately, especially if we are burdened by our guilt and cannot shake that burden. Then a private time of confession will be important for us to hear those words directed very personally to us. After one such private confession, a woman stood with happy tears in her eyes and said, "I feel a hundred pounds lighter!"

But sometimes it will be the neighbor, the brother or sister, who has sinned against us. It will be as if we stood inside and heard that person crying to be let in. Then it becomes our duty to use that key on Christ's behalf—to unlock the door for the penitent willingly and lovingly, or to keep it locked when someone refuses to apologize, refuses to change, and says a stubborn "No!"

Could locking that door actually help someone? Years ago a young boy was angry with his parents for punishing him when he disobeyed. He wanted to defy them and hurt them back, so he decided not to come in for supper when they called. Instead, he hid outside for a long time without budging or speaking. Soon it grew dark and cold, and the rest of the family went on with supper. The boy decided he wanted to come back in, to be fed and get warm. But when he tried the door, he discovered that his parents had locked it. The family was eating without him! After several minutes of knocking and pleading, he saw the door open at last. His father looked at him and asked, "Why are you outside?" When the boy finally confessed his angry rebellion, the father paused and then spoke very deliberately, "Well, then, you may come back in. But don't do that again!"

The good news of the Gospel is that there is love in God's house. The love of Christ that cares for us in our rebellion, and patiently, persistently calls us first to a change of heart and then to return to the table. His love unlocks the door.

When those keys are used for us, or by us, the Lord Jesus himself is at work to bring us home. Come, child. He is waiting for us at the table.

Office of the Keys Two – "Tough Love"

This morning's sermon is about love. All of us are used to hearing about love, especially the sort in poems and love songs that say, "Can't take my eyes off of you" and "I'm falling head over heels." Romantic love. Courtship and marriage kind of love.

But no. I'm not preaching about romance. The love I hold before you this morning is a different sort. A difficult kind of love. A love that at times looks more cruel than kind.

It's been called tough love, because it's tough to *give*, and even tougher to *receive* in the right spirit. Few people nowadays come close to mastering it or even attempting it. It goes by other names, like admonishing or rebuking. Whatever you call it, it is always hard to do.

In fact, I wouldn't try to preach about it all if it weren't for the fact that Jesus himself commanded us to practice it. He said in Matthew 18:15: "If your brother sins against you, go and show him his fault between you and him alone. If he listens to you, you have won your brother over." Jesus obviously thought tough love was important. It behooves us to consider it carefully.

Let's begin by asking very personally, when was the last time someone other than a family member rebuked you, lovingly, for a sin you committed? We might turn that around and ask, when was the last time *you* went to a Christian friend, with loving intent, to confront him or her about some sin?

Honestly, it doesn't happen very often among us. Most people think a rebuke is something one hurls at an enemy, not a service one performs for a friend. Friendship in society these days rarely allows room for rebuke. The result? Many people drifting away from God have no one to bring them back.

Office of the Keys Two – "Tough Love"

Let's take a long look at tough love this morning, letting Matthew 18:15 be our springboard. Notice first that the people with whom we are called to practice such tough love are not merely *friends* but *brothers*. "If your brother sins against you" is how Jesus frames it. Friends often ignore each other's faults, but brothers must live together. They are responsible for each other in a way that friends are not. I am "my brother's keeper" (Gen 4:9). And so are you.

The second thing to notice in this verse is that this love is tough because it deals with a very unpleasant topic: sin. "If your brother sins," says Jesus, "show him his fault." Do we take sin seriously enough to confront it? Do we regard it as a deadly thing that can ruin a life and destroy a church family?

Years ago I heard a story about a family that kept a large python as a pet. There was a tiny toddler in the family, and one day the unthinkable happened. Somehow the snake escaped from its cage, found the unguarded infant, and suffocated that poor child.

Sin operates that way among us. We are aware of the presence of sin in our homes and churches—lying, lust, slander, greed, and more. We shrug and say, "Nobody's perfect," and go on about our business. The sin is allowed to settle in among us, like a pet snake. We make jokes about it, learn to live with it in the next room.

Meanwhile these pet sins quietly wrap themselves about our throats and begin, ever so slowly, to choke the spiritual life out of us. "Your iniquities have separated you from your God," declares Isaiah (Isa 59:2). "The wages of sin is death," warns Paul (Rom. 6:23). Unless they are removed—forcefully—our sins will strangle us.

That's where you and I come into the picture. In most cases, the only thing that stands between a person and his besetting sin is another person who isn't afraid to say something to him. Do we take sin seriously enough to say something?

That is the third point about tough love. It says something. "Go and show him his fault," Jesus directs. That's tough to do. How much easier to keep quiet. To say nothing and look the other way. But have you noticed that if you see someone commit the same sin repeatedly with no apparent awareness of it or any willingness to change, you will begin to despise him? There may be someone about whom you say, "You know, I can't stand to be around so-and-so because I don't like what she does. I have lost my respect for her."

If so, ask yourself, "How is she supposed to change?" Someone should say something to her, shouldn't they?

As a matter of fact, most of us do say something—to the wrong person! The fourth point Jesus makes about tough love is that it is to be directed, first, to the sinner himself. "If your brother sins . . . show him his fault." Him, not someone else.

Is that what we normally do? Or do we pass it along the community grapevine? "Isn't that disgusting?" we tell one another, "I wish someone would straighten him out!"

"You do it," says Jesus. It is the only way to eliminate the degrading gossip that pervades many a church. But many of us will respond, "That's the pastor's job. He can take care of it." One pastor commented that he felt like a large dog which people were continually "siccing" on others.

But who will do it when the pastor himself needs correction?

No, says Jesus. You do it. "Go and show your brother his fault . . . between the two of you." It will show him that you respect his privacy. It will force you to think and pray carefully about what you are to say. And it will seek to move him, not by a show of force, but by your love for him.

Does tough love work? Ah, sometimes it does, says Jesus. "If he listens to you, you have won your brother over." During World War II there were two navy chaplains who were upset about the foul language aboard their ship. The Protestant chaplain gathered the sailors together and berated them at great length. The result? The language got worse. The Roman Catholic chaplain took another tack. He began going to the men one by one. "I respect you," he said to each man, "and I respect God. I sure wish you wouldn't talk about my boss that way!" His plea won them over. The language changed.

But it doesn't always work out like that. "If he listens," says Jesus. But sometimes he won't. Sometimes, no matter how thoughtful or how loving is our attempt to confront and correct a sinning brother, we run into a stone wall. We may be resented, even hated, by the sinner himself, or by his family and friends. "Who do you think you are?" "Let me tell you about your faults . . ."

In truth, a congregation that attempts to practice Christ's brand of tough love, that encourages people to admonish one another and exercises church discipline, will arouse some hostility and may lose some members. Love like he does, and the going will be tough.

Office of the Keys Two – "Tough Love"

By now, I would guess, there may be no one here who wants to obey this command, to love with this kind of love. It sounds too forbidding.

Ah, but there is one thing I have not told you yet. When Jesus concluded giving these instructions, he added a promise in verse 20: "Where two or three are gathered in my name, there am I in the midst of them."

Tough love is not only possible, but it will bear fruit, because Jesus himself will be present and working there, bringing his own Word of forgiveness and healing to his church.

Many years ago at a church in the Midwest, a very young pastor got a phone call on Monday morning from an elderly parishioner. She asked to see him privately. They agreed to meet in the empty sanctuary. He had no idea what she wanted, but her desire for privacy soon became clear. "Yesterday, pastor," she said quietly, "I heard you say something unkind about someone." She repeated what she had heard him say, and in that moment the forgotten conversation rushed back into his mind. He felt ashamed and stung by her truthful words. She went on, "Another pastor I knew made a habit of talking about others like that, and it damaged his ministry. I don't want it to happen to you."

Her words were not only tough, but loving. In that moment he admitted the truth of what she had heard and asked her to forgive him and pray for him to guard his mouth. She did it graciously, sharing a word of pardon from the Bible with him. Then she returned home. That moment of private confession and absolution, the pastor later told colleagues, impacted him from that moment on. He never forgot her courage in showing such tough and helpful love. And he was careful ever after to guard his tongue.

If you have been a Christian very long, he has done the same for you—humbling you, helping you see yourself in the mirror, leading you to a moment of tearful repentance and sweet forgiveness.

Tough love. It's tough, all right, but few things are so urgently important between people who care about each other. It's what makes Weight Watchers work. It's the secret of success in Alcoholics Anonymous. People with a common problem band together to be accountable, to take responsibility for their actions, and to help one another to be healed.

That's God's design for his church. The Lord's brother, James, summed it up this way: "Confess your sins to each other, and pray for each other, so that you may be healed" (Jas 5:16).

Brothers and sisters, we all have a common problem in our sin. And we have a Lord who is bigger than our problem. That's why he came among us. That's why he was named Jesus, because he came to save his people from their sins.

Jesus loves you. Jesus loves me. This we know, for the Bible tells us so. Let's love one another deeply, deliberately, with the tough love by which he sets us free.

The Sacrament of the Altar

The Sacrament of the Altar One - "Holy Communion"

Our text is 1 Corinthians 10:14–17 (KJV). "Wherefore, my dearly beloved, flee from idolatry. I speak as to wise men; judge ye what I say. The cup of blessing which we bless, is it not the communion of the blood of Christ? The bread which we break, is it not the communion of the body of Christ? For we being many are one bread, and one body: for we are all partakers of that one bread."

We have gathered for a meal in which Jesus is the host and we are the guests. It is a meal with a deceptively simple menu: bread and wine. But the variety of names by which it is called reveals a mysterious depth and importance for us Christians.

Some call it the Eucharist, a word that means "Thanksgiving" and stresses the joy we experience here. Some call it The Lord's Supper, reminding themselves that the risen Lord Jesus is our host and is present with us in a special way as we eat. The Small Catechism calls it The Sacrament of the Altar, fixing our gaze on the table where the elements are spread.

In our church the most common name for this meal is Holy Communion. That's the name based on Paul's description of this meal to the Corinthians: "The cup of blessing which we bless, is it not the communion of the blood of Christ? The bread which we break, is it not the communion of the body of Christ?"

Before we take part in this meal, think about that with me. Paul was asking the Corinthians a question in his letter. With whom shall I have this intimate connection, this communion?

It was an important question in Corinth, for Corinth was a seaport city—a melting pot of peoples with a smorgasbord of religions arrayed before them. "Which of those religions is true?" the people must have wondered. "Which one will offer me a genuine 'communion,' a real connection with God?"

Modern America is very like old Corinth. We're a melting-pot nation. Waves of immigrants have washed ashore over centuries. My own ancestors from Germany arrived in the 1840s. But they weren't the first, or the last. There were Englishmen, Italians and Irishmen. There were blacks from Africa brought as slaves, Chinese who came to work on the railroads, and Vietnamese refugees from the war in Southeast Asia. Just lately there are millions of Latinos streaming across our southern border, fueling a great public debate about what we shall do with them all.

America is a land of many peoples and many choices. Too many! We go through life here as one travels through a cafeteria line, dazzled by a bewildering array of opinions, lifestyles, and religions. In America one can see Buddhist shrines, Muslim minarets and Sikh temples alongside the scores of denominations of Christian churches.

We've begun to approach matters of faith and morals as if we were computers with plugs. Increasingly, people shift beliefs and loyalties as easily as we plug and unplug our computers. We plug in to a congregation. If unhappy, we unplug and go elsewhere.

Such an approach to religion may be convenient, but over the long haul, its results are disastrous for real community. People are experiencing a growing sense of detachment, a restlessness and a rootlessness. "Where," disconnected people ask, "can I find a connection with God and with other people?"

Find it here, writes Paul, in this meal. This meal is a call to abandon the "plug-in" mentality and experience a lasting communion with God and community with people. A communion and a community that is deep, not casual; permanent, not temporary.

It is like the union begun in marriage. There, two people become one. Not merely friends who like each other's company, but "one flesh." Just so, here in this meal, we are invited to be united with Jesus Christ, with his body, his blood, himself.

The Greek word translated "communion" is *koinonia*, which means "to have a share in" something, like one has a slice of a pie. Here at Communion, we do not simply think about Jesus. We actually "take part in" and "have a share of" Jesus himself. As we do it, we receive the benefits he offers. In his Small Catechism, Luther lists them simply: "forgiveness of sins, life, and salvation."[1]

---

1. Luther, *Small Catechism*, 31

The Sacrament of the Altar One - "Holy Communion"

We come to Holy Communion so often, so routinely. How often do we stop to consider what is happening here? To put it another way, do we take seriously the union that is implied and offered to us in this communion? We cannot simply plug in for a few moments, then unplug as if nothing happened here.

Our communion with God can't be forgotten once we hit the parking lot or the bedroom or the bowling alley, any more than a newly-married couple can forget the vows they spoke at the altar last year. When times get tough, they will remember "for better or worse . . . in sickness and in health . . . till death do us part."

Here is the Gospel in this meal: at this Communion table, our Lord takes the part of the Bridegroom, and gives us the very thing he demands, total devotion. "Take and eat my body for you, my blood for you."

But Paul said more. There is another dimension in this meal. Communion with Christ yields a communion with one another. It would be possible, wouldn't it, as we come to the altar, to be so focused on the sacredness of this moment and our relationship with God that we feel almost disturbed by the presence of other people, especially those with whom we have quarreled in the kitchen or the committee meeting. But that person, the bothersome one, is one of the very reasons we are invited to come to this meal. How else are we to reconcile, to become one?

We are so very different, he and I! He is young. I am old. He is single. I am married. We work different jobs, and we have such different opinions, especially in our political views. Apart from this meal, and this common Lord, what do we have in common? But when we come and stand together here, everything changes.

Like the spokes of a wheel, we are joined in the center—in Christ. Paul says, "we, being many, are one bread and one body." Quite literally, we are sharing Christ. That has a lot to say to us at those moments when we find ourselves feuding and fussing and wishing that old so-and-so would find some other church, or just disappear! What in the world do I have in common with that person?

This meal is God's answer. Our unity does not depend on all of us looking alike or thinking alike. It depends on the one Christ we are sharing. Come to this meal, and God will join our hands, bridge our quarrels, and make us one.

Or will we dare to come to this meal and hang on to those old grudges, that old bitterness? I remember vividly one Communion celebration at Concordia Seminary in 1972. I was in my final year there, and I was newly a father. That morning I had gotten into a quarrel with another student at breakfast in the cafeteria. We parted with frowns on our faces, leaving things unresolved.

Scarcely two hours later, we all stood outdoors in the open quadrangle, preparing to receive Holy Communion at our chapel time. The words of institution were spoken, as usual. Then the presiding professor turned, looked at us for a moment, and quoted a brief section from Matthew's Gospel: "Therefore, if you are offering your gift at the altar and there remember that your brother has something against you, leave your gift there in front of the altar. First go and be reconciled to your brother; then come and offer your gift" (Matt 5:23–24).

"Gentlemen," he said, "I want you to do that now." Then he waited. I knew what I had to do. There was my breakfast table opponent across the way. I sheepishly made my way to him. I apologized. We shook hands. Then we ate. That day I learned the importance of the union in our communion. The union of the repentant. The union of those forgiven by Jesus and forgiving each other.

That is His invitation to you tonight. Come. Enjoy a fellowship, a communion with God—a moment like no other. And as you do, discover again the communion with each other that breaks all barriers, heals all wounds, and joins all who are divided.

The meal is ready. Our Host says, "Come."

Sacrament of the Altar Two - "Getting Ready for the Supper"

ALL OF US HAVE been asked, "Are you ready yet?" The answer depends on what you're getting ready for.

Children know what their parents mean by that question. Being ready for school means being dressed, having your books in your backpack, having a lunch packed (or at least lunch money), and being on time to catch the bus. Being ready for bed means having your room straightened up, teeth brushed, pajamas on, and prayers said.

We adults must be ready too. Ready to head to work. Ready for a long-planned vacation trip. Ready for tax time, which means rummaging through our financial records and making sure we have our W-2s and 1099s. If there comes a big event like a wedding, there's the schedule to check, a gift to buy, and a card to write.

For us Christians, there is no bigger event than the meal we are about to share here at church. It's not just any meal. It is the Lord's Supper, the holiest thing we do together. C. S. Lewis considered the sacrament the "holiest object presented to your senses."[1] So important is what happens here that careful thought and prayerful preparation are vital. Martin Luther wrote in the Large Catechism, "We do not intend to grant admission . . . to those who do not know what they are looking for or why they are coming."[2]

First Corinthians chapter 11 is a window through which we are invited to look at a congregation that was not ready for the holy supper and had serious trouble because of it. Let's look at it together so that we might be well-prepared and receive the nourishment God intends for us.

---

1. Lewis, The Weight of Glory, 15
2. Luther, *Large Catechism,* 110.

Here's the text, verses 20–30: "So then, when you come together, it is not the Lord's Supper you eat, for when you are eating, some of you go ahead with your own private suppers. As a result, one person remains hungry and another gets drunk. Don't you have homes to eat and drink in? Or do you despise the church of God by humiliating those who have nothing? What shall I say to you? Shall I praise you? Certainly not in this matter! For I received from the Lord what I also passed on to you: The Lord Jesus, on the night he was betrayed, took bread, and when he had given thanks, he broke it and said, 'This is my body, which is for you; do this in remembrance of me.' In the same way, after supper he took the cup, saying, 'This cup is the new covenant in my blood; do this, whenever you drink it, in remembrance of me.' For whenever you eat this bread and drink this cup, you proclaim the Lord's death until he comes. So then, whoever eats the bread or drinks the cup of the Lord in an unworthy manner will be guilty of sinning against the body and blood of the Lord. Everyone ought to examine themselves before they eat of the bread and drink from the cup. For those who eat and drink without discerning the body of Christ eat and drink judgment on themselves. That is why many among you are weak and sick, and a number of you have fallen asleep."

The congregation in Corinth thought they were having the Lord's Supper. They were meeting and eating, weren't they? They checked off the box, satisfied with themselves. But Paul was distressed with the reports that had filtered back to him about their worship life. "Your meetings do more harm than good," he concluded. That must have raised some eyebrows! His concern was focused on the "unworthy manner" in which they conducted their sacramental meals.

"It is not the Lord's Supper you eat," was his stunning evaluation. The problem was not the "potluck" setting, which was common practice among the Christians of that time. People brought food for a community meal like our potlucks. The food was to be shared as an expression of Christian love. But in their case the focus was not on sharing, but on self-indulgence. "As you eat," he told them, "each of you goes ahead without waiting for anybody else. One remains hungry. Another gets drunk."

What was designed to be a worship service had devolved into a sloppy, selfish frat party there in Corinth. The rich folks stuffed themselves, while the poor folks looked on, hungry and humiliated. "What shall I say to you," asked Paul rhetorically. "Shall I praise you for this?" He answers his own question: "Certainly not!" Paul was angry with them, and distressed about

Sacrament of the Altar Two - "Getting Ready for the Supper"

where it was leading. Such selfishness lost sight of what the church was to be—the "body of the Lord," that holy fellowship. Result? The church was splintered into factions!

Selfishness toward other believers was bad enough. Even worse was the heedlessness toward the meal itself and what God was providing them in it. Their careless and selfish indulgence blinded them. They were eating and drinking "without recognizing the body of the Lord" in another way—not seeing the body and blood of Christ present under the bread and wine. The result was not a sacrament, but a sacrilege. They were "sinning against the body and blood of the Lord."

Already Paul could see that it was having dire effects in Corinth. "That is why many among you are weak and sick, and a number of you have fallen asleep." The outbreak of sickness at Corinth and the deaths of several could rightly be read as the judgment of God. It's a sobering thought for us who are inclined to minimize the seriousness of such a careless approach to worship and the sacrament.

Accordingly, Paul offers some pastoral advice to them that we need to hear still today. For there is a way to get ready for this holy meal. We could summarize his advice in three words: remember, reflect, and respect.

First, remember! This meal was instituted by Jesus himself. Back to the Upper Room he takes them, back to the Last Supper. Listen again to his words, Paul says: "The Lord Jesus ... took bread ... and said, 'This is my body, which is for you ... ' In the same way ... he took the cup, saying, 'this cup is the new covenant in my blood ... do this ... in remembrance of me.'"

The proper preparation, Luther explained, is not *outward*, but *inward*. "Fasting and bodily preparation are certainly fine outward training," he wrote in the Small Catechism. "But that person is truly worthy and well prepared who has faith in these words: 'Given and shed for you for the forgiveness of sins.'"[3] So each Sunday we begin by remembering the words of Jesus. The pastor speaks them. We hear and take them to heart.

Are we remembering those words today?

The second preparation is to reflect on ourselves and our need for the meal. Paul put it this way: "Let a man examine himself." In the church we confess our sins, something similar to the way Alcoholics Anonymous calls for a "fearless and searching moral inventory." Here again we may use the mirror of God's Word. Years ago pastors urged their students to employ the Ten Commandments as the mirror. To have communion without

---

3. Luther, *Small Catechism*, 31

confession, Dietrich Bonhoeffer warned, is to cheapen God's grace and make us careless like the Corinthians.[4]

Do we get listless and lazy about desiring this meal? Luther advised that if a person felt no need for the sacrament, "I can give you no better counsel than to tell you to pinch yourselves and see if you are still flesh and blood."[5] If you are, he adds, then believe what God's Word tells you about your flesh and its sinful need.

Are we reflecting honestly, humbly about ourselves and our desperate need?

Finally, as we remember Christ's Word and reflect on our sins, we will respect our neighbor who comes to kneel beside us. "Wait for each other," he says simply. Wait on each other, for you have a common humanity. Be thankful that you are not alone, but part of a community, each one loved and welcomed by Jesus Christ. Mend your quarrels, so that nothing will hinder him or you from taking part in this holy meal. Welcome the lowly like dear siblings.

Remember. Reflect. Respect. That is how to get ready. Come trustingly, believing what God tells us he offers here. Come humbly, knowing our hunger and need for it. Come respectfully, seeing each other as brothers and sisters gathered round the family table.

In so doing we will be well prepared to receive this holy meal.

---

4. Bonhoeffer, *Cost of Discipleship*, 47
5. Luther, *Large Catechism*, 119–20.

Bibliography

Alcorn, Randy. *Heaven*. Wheaton: Tyndale House, 2004.
Alighieri, Dante. *The Divine Comedy*. Tr. by Henry Wadsworth Longfellow. Project Gutenberg. https://www.gutenberg.org/ebooks/1003.
Attenborough, Richard, dir. *Gandhi*. Columbia Pictures, 1982.
Augustine, of Hippo, Saint, 354-430. *The Confessions of St. Augustine*. Tr. by Rex Warner. New York: The New American Library, 1963.
Biedriczky, Bartek. "Did Comrade Gagarin See God in Space?" Medium. Apr. 12, 2021. https://worldsnest.medium.com/did-comrade-gagarin-see-god-in- space
Bonhoeffer, Dietrich. *The Cost of Discipleship*. New York: Macmillan, 1966.
———. *Life Together*. San Francisco: Harper and Row, 1954.
Cameron, James, dir. *Titanic*. Paramount Pictures, 1997.
Christianity Stack Exchange. "Where Did Martin Luther Say?" Feb. 16, 2019. https://christianity.stackexchange.com/questions/68678/where-did-martin-luther-say.
"Effects of Out-of-Wedlock Births on Society." Marripedia. https://marripedia.org/effects of out-of-wedlock births on society.
Forsberg, Rolf, dir. *The Antkeeper*. Gospel Films Archive, 1966.
Graham, Billy. *How to be Born Again*. Nashville: Thomas Nelson, 1989.
Jastrow, Robert. *God and the Astronomers*. New York: W. W. Norton, 1978.
Christian Quotes. "Martin Lloyd-Jones on Forgiveness." http://christian-quotes.ochristian.com/christian-quotes_ochristian.cgi?find=Christian-quotes-by-Martyn+Lloyd-Jones-on-Forgiveness#google_vignette.
Kantor, McKinley. *Andersonville*. Cleveland: World, 1955.
Klobuchar, Jim. "You Killed My Husband; I Forgive." *Minneapolis Star*, Sept. 9, 1970. Page 9.
Kurz, Joel. "Why Being Lutheran Matters Today: a Review of A. Trevor Sutton's *Being Lutheran*." The Cresset. Vol. LXXX, No. 2 (Advent-Christmas) 2016.
Lewis, C. S. *Christian Reflections*. Grand Rapids: Eerdmans, 1967.
———. *Mere Christianity*. New York: Macmillan, 1977.
———. *The Screwtape Letters*. New York: Macmillan, 1968.
———. *The Weight of Glory and Other Addresses*. Grand Rapids: Eerdmans, 1965.
Luther, Martin. *Luther's Large Catechism: A Contemporary Translation with Study Questions*. Tr. by F. Samuel Janzow. St. Louis: Concordia, 1978.
———. *Luther's Small Catechism with Explanation*. St. Louis: Concordia, 1986.
———. Third Sermon for Easter Day, Torgau, 1533. Emmanuel Lutheran Church Newsletter. Las Cruces, New Mexico. May 3, 2023.

Bibliography

Maier, Paul. *First Easter: the True and Unfamiliar Story in Words and Pictures.* New York: Harper and Row, 1973.

Mohler, Albert. "Looking Forward, Looking Back: A Conversation with Historian Martin E. Marty." AlbertMohler.com, Mar. 7, 2011. https://albertmohler.com/2011/03/03/looking-forward-looking-back-a-conversation-with-historian-martin-e-marty.

Moody, Raymond. *Life after Life.* New York: Random House, 2001.

Peterson, Eugene. *Under the Unpredictable Plant: an Exploration in Vocational Holiness.* Grand Rapids: Eerdmans, 1992.

Pirandello, Luigi. *Six Characters in Search of an Author.* Mineola: Dover, 2012.

Quoist, Michel. *Prayers.* New York: Sheed and Ward, 1963.

Quote Investigator. "When I Was a Boy of Fourteen, My Father Was So Ignorant." Oct. 10, 2010. https://quoteinvestigator.com/2010/10/10/twain-father/#google_vignette.

"Sexually Transmitted Infections." Pan American Health Organization. https://www.paho.org/en/topics/sexually-transmitted-infections.

"Sexually Transmitted Infections Prevalence, Incidence, and Cost Estimates in the United States." Centers for Disease Control, Apr. 23, 2024. https://www.cdc.gov/sti/php/communication-resources/prevalence-incidence-and-cost-estimates.html.

Shakespeare, William. *The Tragedy of Romeo and Juliet.* Folger Shakespeare Library. Ed. by Barbara Mowat and Paul Werstine. New York: Simon and Schuster, 2011.

Simmons, Carl. "Rediscovering Our Reverence." Lay It Down. Dec. 11, 2015. https://carlsimmonslive.com/2015/12/11/rediscovering-our-reverence/.

"Smalcald Articles." *The Book of Concord.* Tr. and ed. by T. G. Tappert. Philadelphia: Muhlenberg, 1959.

Sneed, Michael. "Why Chicago's First Female Mayor Moved into the City's Most Notorious Housing Project." Chicago Sun Times. Mar. 6, 2020. https://chicago.suntimes.com/columnists/2020/3/6/21168138/michael-sneed-cabrini-green-jane-byrne-housing-projects-apartment-416-lookingglass-theatre.

"Suicide Prevention." Centers for Disease Control. cdc.gov/suicide/facts/index.html.

Tim Gaiser MS Blog. "Why Geography Matters." Apr. 18, 2016. https://timgaiser.com/blog/why-geography-matters/.

Thielicke, Helmut. *I Believe: the Christian's Creed.* Tr. By John W. Doberstein and H. George Anderson. Philadelphia: Fortress, 1968.

———. *Our Heavenly Father: Sermons on the Lord's Prayer.* Grand Rapids: Baker, 1974.

Tolstoy, Leo. *How Much Land Does a Man Need? And Other Stories.* London: Penguin, 1994.

Warren, Rick. *The Purpose-Driven Life.* Grand Rapids: Zondervan, 2002.

Washington University in St. Louis. "'I Know it When I See it': A History of Obscenity and Pornography in the United States." 2024. https://history.wustl.edu/i-know-it-when-i-see-it-history-obscenity-pornography-united-states.

Wildsmith, Elizabeth et al., "Dramatic Increases in the Proportion of Births Outside of Marriage in the United States from 1990 to 2016." Child Trends. Aug. 8, 2018. https://www.childtrends.org/publications/dramatic-increase-in- percentage- of-births-outside-marriage-among-whites-hispanics-and-women-with-higher-education-levels.

Williams, Allison. "The Ancient Spirit That Settled in Small-Town Washington." Seattle Met. Nov. 15, 2022. https://www.seattlemet.com/news-and-city-life/2022/11/jz-knight-ramtha-yelm-washington-school-of-enlightenment.

Wunderlich, Lorenz. *The Half-Known God.* St. Louis: Concordia, 1963.

www.ingramcontent.com/pod-product-compliance
Lightning Source LLC
Chambersburg PA
CBHW071426160426
43195CB00013B/1826